Foolosophy

Humor is The Key to a Healthy Mind

By Darrell Ruocco

20660 Stevens Creek Blvd.
Suite 210
Cupertino, CA 95014

Copyright © 2007 by Happy About®

All rights reserved. No part of this book shall be reproduced, stored in a retrieval system, or transmitted by any means electronic, mechanical, photocopying, recording, or otherwise without written permission from the publisher. No patent liability is assumed with respect to the use of the information contained herein. Although every precaution has been taken in the preparation of this book, the publisher and author(s) assume no responsibility for errors or omissions. Neither is any liability assumed for damages resulting from the use of the information contained herein.

First Printing: September, 2007
Paperback ISBN: 1600050573 (978-1-60005-057-2)
Place of Publication: Silicon Valley, California, USA
Paperback Library of Congress Number: 2007936276

eBook ISBN: 1600050581 (978-1-60005-058-9)

Trademarks

All terms mentioned in this book that are known to be trademarks or service marks have been appropriately capitalized. Happy About® cannot attest to the accuracy of this information. Use of a term in this book should not be regarded as affecting the validity of any trademark or service mark.

Warning and Disclaimer

Every effort has been made to make this book as complete and as accurate as possible, but no warranty of fitness is implied. The information provided is on an "as is" basis. The authors and the publisher shall have neither liability nor responsibility to any person or entity with respect to an loss or damages arising from the information contained in this book. Some characters have been fictionalized to protect the innocent or, in this case, potentially the not so innocent.

Praise for 'Foolosophy'

"Will Rogers, Groucho Marx, Woody Allen, Deepak Chopra. Darrell Ruocco is taller than all of them."
Ray Abruzzo AKA Little Carmine Lupertazzi, THE SOPRANOS

"Darryl totally gets it: not only is laughter the best medicine, it leaves you with the most flattering wrinkles."
Wendie Malick, Actress/Activist

"In my toughest of competitions when things weren't going the best for me, all I needed to do was think of Ruocco and Foolosophy and all the pressure would disappear. This is when that mysterious smile would grace my face and confuse my opponents. This guaranteed me many a victory."
Sinjin Smith, Olympian and World Champion

"Just the word 'Foolosophy' makes me laugh, and I agree with Darrell that humor is the spirits best friend!"
Liz Masakayan, Indoor Volleyball Olympian and Beach Volleyball World Champion

"'Foolosophy' is music playing in my head that feeds me on many levels. Reading this book will help feed what's in your head!"
Frank Stallone, Singer-Songwriter, Actor

"After I read about Foolosophy I was so aggrevated and ashamed about how much of my life has been spent as an institutionalized robot; now I just laugh about it."
Susie, 22- year old, Ivy League Graduate Psych Major

"Ruocco's book (that he charged me full retail price for) showed me how much of a putz I've been all these years. From one foolish putz to another- thanks D."
Sid, 58-year old, Retired Noodge

"Even after reading Foolosophy and laughing out loud, I still cannot laugh at myself; but at least now I'm trying to."
John, 32-year old, Graphic Artist and Crumudgen

"The wisdom of Foolosophy gives me more energy and bursts of spontaneous creativity; it allows me the freedom to move and dance wildly without fear of embarassment."
Michelle, 40-year old, Ballroom Dance Instructor and Former Gold-digger

"My friends and I pass around Foolosophy at school, and then we quiz each other about it. We have even developed our own Foolosophy language as our secret code."
Nick, 15-year old, High School Student/Burnout

"The Foolish humor of Darrell's book assists me in all of my daily arbitrations; most of all, with my humorless ex-wife."
Walter, 47-year old, Divorce Attorney/Screenwriter

"I found a copy of the book in my dumpster; it smells pretty funny."
Roscoe, 77-year old, Former Mr. Olympia and Currently an Auto Detailer

"Reading this book made me so emotional; it brought back so many memories of my children's youth, and the joy of growing up with the foolish will of a child."
Virginia, 50-year old, Stay-at-Home Mother of 3 and Part-time Day-Trader

"I read the Foolosophy book until it ended."
Jon Dubin, 45-year old, Foolosopher and Writer

Dedicated to the Human Race (What a disgrace!)

Success/Failure

"Mistake -- Nothing more than experimental success."
Thomas Edison

If you can develop your sense of humor and learn to laugh at yourself daily, I guarantee you will feel like the most successful person on Earth. The only problem with this advice is it is coming to you from the biggest fool/failure that ever lived. But in my mind, it only proves how effective humor and laughing at oneself can be to overcome everything in life, even our own thoughts and feeling of being worthless. It is the beautiful expression coined on Saturday Night Live (SNL), "I'm not worthy..." In foolosophy, everyone is worthy of being laughed at with the proper love and intention.

Foolosophy is humanity's coming out party and everyone tells me it is time for a shift to a higher consciousness beyond our five senses. The two primary senses in foolosophy are our sense of play and our sense of humor which takes us back to the roots of our greatness...

Acknowledgements

For my beloved parents Victoria and Jack Ruocco who always allowed me and my brother Ron to practice using humor and mimicry on them as well as all others who entered our home growing up.

Much appreciation to Dr. Lisa Stiller, Dr. John Casey, Brian (Miracle Boy) Visintin, Russ (Bad Boy Buddha) Kizior, Jon Dubin. And to my publisher, Mitchell Levy, who through his efforts made my parents cry.

A big thanks to Rob (J.C.) Ingersoll and Jenny Flores for cover picture and bringing up the rear.

Special thanks to the hundreds of characters I've had the good fortune and bad fortune to know for it has been in the diversity, duality, pain and joy of playing with all my fellow freaks, fools, geniuses and nuts, that the real fun is to be had.

Who am I?

My business card reads: The Comedy Therapist. People have always been my inspiration and motivation. They get me high, and humor helps me stay in this heavenly state of consciousness. This is no joke, and I do not tell jokes. I use humor and laughter to open people's minds, repair their broken hearts, and to free the childlike spirit that resides in us all.

You may stop taking pills, stop using drugs, alcohol, and spend a lot less time with your psychotherapist by using your innate, instinctual sense of humor. Every child born on Earth, therefore every human being has humor within them, thus, the ability to laugh and liberate themselves. If you don't believe me, just watch children at play. Remember fall down, go boom? We children of the world rise up laughing, eager to resume our playful, fun-seeking ways. Short of a really bad fall, which brings a lot of pain, we are resilient, durable, curious, fearless maniacs, hungry to learn how to develop our physical, mental, and social skills, within own unique personality.

Here are two beautiful thoughts from the great Mark Twain: "It takes a heap of sense to write good nonsense," and "Against the assault of laughter nothing can stand."

Don't let the title of this book, or anything else in this book, FOOL YOU! This may be the most important book written about the key to keeping you and I most important. In my short lifetime I have witnessed human beings becoming less and less important which has caused me a ton of pain. But it is only because I know pain so intimately and can howl at the insanity that surrounds us that I have kept from checking out like all the other highly sensitive, intelligent, caring people before me.

Humor is the word, the name we have attached to the function of our magical little brain assisting us in adapting and adjusting to a world that makes no sense to us much of the time. It is the prepared mind which allows us to look at the things that make no sense to us, reflect upon them for a time (we all have different and varied time tables of reflection), discover that very few things make any sense at all, shake our head side-to-side therefore shaking off our limited understanding, converting it all back into total nonsense, so we can bravely laugh at the things that we cannot always comprehend. Courage wants us to laugh, and humor is designed to make us fearless so that we may fully live.

Short of a serious clinical, mental, and/or chemical imbalance, humor is the best natural healer we human beings have available to us. Humor is not a Western thing or an Eastern thing; it's a most human thing. Take advantage of your most important sense, for the advantages of humor are endless and eternal...

- **NOTE:** *If you do mind me saying so, then please buy a second copy of this book and read it side-by-side with a friend who does have a sense of humor. Go over it thoroughly until you learn to find the humor in you.*

Another Warning

The following book may contain sensitive information subject to misinterpretation by untrained individuals. Our intention is not to offend anyone, however, please allow us the latitude to flush out the most important tool for survival, education, getting everything you want, keeping everything you have, getting the guy, getting the girl, understanding mom and dad, brother, sister, everyone in school, everyone out of school, and everyone you meet. This is not a joke. Having fun is serious business. The secrets to life regarding fun, play, silliness, and a well developed sense of humor are contained within this book, and if taken as intended, will result in a "Renaissance of Fun"...

What Little I Know Is A Lot

I never learned anything from being right, only from being wrong
I never learned anything from winning, only from losing
I never learned anything from pleasure, only from pain
I never learned anything from love, only from hate
I may be the most intelligent person on Earth
For I never let my intellect or ego get in the way of a good time
Foolosophy is the confidence to laugh at oneself
Which is the shortcut to loving oneself
Sound like fun? You have no idea...

A Message From Happy About®

Thank you for your purchase of this Happy About book. It is available online at http://happyabout.info/foolosophy.php or at other online and physical bookstores.

- Please contact us for quantity discounts at sales@happyabout.info
- If you want to be informed by e-mail of upcoming Happy About® books, please e-mail bookupdate@happyabout.info

Happy About is interested in you if you are an author who would like to submit a non-fiction book proposal or a corporation that would like to have a book written for you. Please contact us by e-mail editorial@happyabout.info or phone (1-408-257-3000).

Other Happy About books available include:

- Lessons About Life Momma Never Taught Us
  http://happyabout.info/consumer-books.php
- Jesus Drank, Judas Repented and God Divorced His Bride
  http://happyabout.info/myfaith/jesusdrank.php
- Happy About Working to Stay Young
  http://happyabout.info/working-to-stay-young.php
- Tales From the Networking Community
  http://happyabout.info/networking-community.php
- Happy About Online Networking:
  http://happyabout.info/onlinenetworking.php
- Confessions of a Resilient Entrepreneur:
  http://happyabout.info/confessions-entrepreneur.php
- Memoirs of the Money Lady:
  http://happyabout.info/memoirs-money-lady.php
- 30-Day Bootcamp: Your Ultimate Life Makeover:
  http://happyabout.info/30daybootcamp/life-makeover.php
- Happy About Joint Venturing:
  http://happyabout.info/jointventuring.php

Contents

Foreword	The Backward Foreword 1
Preface	Foolosophy Preface 3
Part I	**Opening Your Comic Mind**. 5
Chapter 1	A New Spiritual Paradigm in the World's Oldest Art Form... 7
	It's All Foolosophy. 8
	Foolosophy Takes the Pressure Off of God. 10
	Humor is the Core of Foolosophy. 11
Chapter 2	Two of the Greatest Foolosophers who Ever Lived... 13
Chapter 3	I Couldn't Care More 15
Chapter 4	I'm Not Kidding. 17
Chapter 5	A Smiling Mind 19
Chapter 6	Bigger, Badder, Better 21
Chapter 7	Television Through Humor's Vision 23
Chapter 8	Love Thy Neighbor. 25
Chapter 9	Developing Your Sense of Humor 27
Chapter 10	Whatever 31

Part II	To Be or Not to Be: Spiritual!	33
Chapter 1	Dalai of the West	35
Chapter 2	Speak for Yourself	37
Chapter 3	Email from Jesus	39
Chapter 4	I'm Tired of Being Angry...	41
Chapter 5	Angry Soul	43
Chapter 6	Pure Silliness	45
Part III	Beautiful Cripple	47
Chapter 1	Beautiful Cripple	49
Chapter 2	The Art of Teasing	51
Chapter 3	Between the Ears	53
Chapter 4	Humor's Balance	57
Chapter 5	Humor's Intervention	59
Chapter 6	There's Definitely Something Wrong With Me	61
Part IV	I Like My Pain Straight	63
Chapter 1	Does My Smile Confuse You?	65
Chapter 2	I'm Dead Serious	69
Chapter 3	Your Royal Insignificance	71
Chapter 4	Mom's Pain / My Pain	73

Chapter 5	Dad's Anger 75
Chapter 6	If Ignorance is Bliss, than is Awareness Painful?.................. 77
Chapter 7	The Last Romantic in Los Angeles....... 79
Chapter 8	Speed Dating 81
Chapter 9	The Rats are Getting Bigger, and the Maze is Getting Smaller......... 83
Chapter 10	Pain Transference 87

Part V	Perception and a Healthy Mind 89
Chapter 1	Has Anyone Seen My Identity?.......... 91
Chapter 2	The Adult Toy....................... 93
Chapter 3	Socio-Pathetic Behavior 95
Chapter 4	Joy Transference 97
Chapter 5	Truth is the Fountain of Youth 101
Chapter 6	A Children's Book for Adults 103
Chapter 7	The Great Healer..................... 105
Chapter 8	Does My Smile Confuse You?.......... 107
Chapter 9	To Know Me is to Love You............ 109
Chapter 10	Humor is it........................ 111
Chapter 11	It is in God's Hands 113
Chapter 12	Programmed and Conditioned 115
Chapter 13	Food For Thought 117

Chapter 14	What Makes a Personality Great?	119
Chapter 15	For Women	121
Part VI	**Life is All Improvisation**	**123**
Chapter 1	Attention	125
Chapter 2	Intention	127
Chapter 3	I'm Just Kidding	129
Chapter 4	Love is All the Confidence You Need	131
Chapter 5	I Love Humor	133
Chapter 6	May I Be Partially Honest With You?	137
Chapter 7	Have an Awful Day	141
Chapter 8	Call Me a Fool	143
Chapter 9	"Fools Anonymous"- 12 Step Program	145
Chapter 10	Exercising One's Personality	149
Chapter 11	Jump For Joy	153
Chapter 1	Conclusion: The Last Laugh	155
Appendix A	Official Foolosophy Dictionary	157
Appendix B	Reading People / Reading Books	169
Books	Other Happy About Books	173

Foreword

The Backward Foreword

This could be the most important book ever written since the Bible and The Little Prince[1]. And it is likewise the most unimportant book ever transcribed following Everyone Poops[2].

Foolosophy is foolproof. It allows us to play the fool, allows us to embrace the fool, and allows us to be fully free while playing the greatest character we can ever be. It's not for the greater good; it's for the greatest good.

If this book doesn't go off the charts as the best seller ever, then it is over for society. I'm not kidding, I'm dead serious. I will be happy to debate anyone dead or alive on Earth about humor being our most important sense, and should I be proved wrong, I will happily enjoy laughing at that discovery.

We are all born with an innate instinctual sense of humor. It's in our DNA and we don't have to wait for science to find the humor gene. Every adult needs to develop this and practice daily the art of laughing at themselves as well as anyone and everyone they want to get close to.

Life is self-education, and the tragedy of all schooling is that no one helps us or teaches us the importance of humor. Up until now we have been on our own to discover this, but maybe this

---

1. The Little Prince by Antoine De Saint-exupery, Harcourt Brace & Company, 1943
2. Everyone Poops by Taro Gomi, Kane/Miller, 2001

book can be the beginning to a new way of educating the public. We are all social emotional creatures and whether we like it or not, we are stuck with one another. So we might as well make all social emotional intercourse more playful, fun, and healthy.

Life is not about proof and validation, yet here I am trying to prove to the world the importance of humor. And because I've spent so long writing, diving deeper into my heart, soul, and psyche trying to bring my baby forward into the world, it almost killed me it caused so much pain and frustration. For brief periods each day I did lose my sense of humor. But I discovered this to be normal, this is to be expected, and what I found to be important is to salvage each day upon reflection and laugh your a-- off at these painful moments.

In all seriosity, humor is the most important thing in the world. In the words of Oscar Wilde, "We must not take life so seriously that we cannot fully live."

Throughout our history, the jester, the tricksters, the clowns, and the great comic minds have made fun of rigidity, small mindedness, and seriousness. For the present, the comedy of existence has not yet become conscious of itself. For the present, we still live in the age of a tragedy. But who wants to live here? Humor does not want to die a slow painful death of heart and soul. It is the head game that makes consciousness a good thing.

Everybody laughs at me when I tell them the book I've been working on is only one page. They keep pushing me with, "No really, how many pages is your book?" Just to prove to you, the reader, that I am the biggest fool who ever lived, what follows this foreword is nothing but filler, because I pretty much said it all on page 1. But so you don't feel cheated, I've supplied the rest of this book for your foolosophical enjoyment. And if you don't enjoy it, then obviously you haven't fully developed your sense of humor yet, therefore my only concern would be, is this book enough?

Preface

Foolosophy Preface

I was unconsciously unaware at the age of seven that I was already developing my sense of humor to help my beloved mother manage and control, her negative thoughts and emotions. This was done by my mirroring back to her, her pained fearful worried expression which made her smile/laugh more quickly, getting her out of her negative state of consciousness. Making my silly faces and mocking mom's pained expressions, helped us both out of an uncomfortable mental place. As a child, mom's unhappy expressions confused me, bewildered me causing me some pain of my own. My sensitivity was killing me. It disturbed me when mom left her playful fun-loving nurturing state of being, so my instincts took over and this was the beginning of my long love affair with this thing we call humor and the magical power of laughter. Humor is not an Eastern thing or a Western thing; it is a most human thing.

This simple story is the key to appreciating and understanding the positive aspects of humor and laughter. I've used humor all my life to help release, free everyone (most importantly myself), from a negative state of unconsciousness. Foolosophy is not about putting another human being down to feel better about oneself. It's the complete opposite. It's about using our individual, collective sense of humor to lift our fellow man, woman, child, out of an unhealthy mental space. This is called friendship, this is called love, this is called caring, this is called sharing, this is called compassion, this is called empathy, and this is humanity at work. Keep this simple yet complex thought in mind as you read this book. If you can use your own sense of humor as you practice lifting everyone you love, or want to get next to, out of a negative space, well, that's foolosophy.

Part I
Opening Your Comic Mind

Every honest slip-up or mistake you make is a positive step towards opening-up your comic mind; in your most inept, embarrassing and frustrating moments you will be given the opportunity to celebrate the comedy of your own life.

After you make a human error or just mess up and play the fool, there is no going back! Nothing can be done except to sincerely laugh at yourself. FOOLOSOPHY is the key ingredient to a comic mind, which is the basis for a healthy mind. A healthy mind is necessary to have a happy heart, and with a happy heart there automatically is liveliness to one's soul!

This step in the "wrong" direction leads to an expedited form of personal maturity and forgiveness that we, as human beings, have to laugh at ourselves for feeling foolish.

Welcome to FOOLOSOPHY!

Chapter 1
A New Spiritual Paradigm in the World's Oldest Art Form...

> *The Fool is not a philosophy, but a quality of consciousness of life, an endless regard for human identity; all this lives in the fun of the Fool. The Fool is the essential poetic integrity of life itself, clear and naked, overflowing in cosmic fun; not the product of intellectual achievement, but a creation of the culture of the heart. A culture of the genius of life. I believe that there is in life, and in the human psyche, a certain quality, an inviolate eternal innocence, and this quality I call the Fool. It is a continuous wisdom and compassion that heals with fun and magic. It is the joy of the original Adam in men.*
>
> **Cecil Collins, The Vision of the Fool**[3]

Foolosophy can best be described as being unafraid of making a fool of yourself, so that you can make a foolosopher of yourself and develop your comic mind, so that you can make yourself infinitely greater at anything you do, while having the most fun in life.

---

3. The Vision of the Fool, by Cecil Collins, The University Of Chicago, 2001

Making a fool of yourself, or someone else making a fool of you, then becomes the cornerstone of foolosophy. And you need not fear it, because the fool is the greatest character you can ever be. He is open, inept, and silly, yet wise beyond ordinary understanding. And you can see the fool anytime you want; he is the one you see everyday when you look into the mirror or walk down the street. William Shakespeare said it best when he said, "Lord, what fools these mortals be."[4] True liberation occurs when you can accept the fool in you. From there the sky is the limit, as your life will begin to spiral upward.

"If the fool would persist in his folly, he would become wise," said the great William Blake[5]. I say, if the fool would persist in his folly he would become a foolosopher. Any fool who can learn through his mistakes is a foolosopher. In fact, it is the mistakes, and anything that lies in the negative that is of the utmost importance to a foolosopher because they know that through pain and negativity comes a chance to further develop their sense of humor. All foolosophers understand that their sense of humor is the most important sense they have because it fuels their sense of play, and a well developed sense of humor and a strong sense of play allow for an advantage over the big game of life. This is the purpose of humor, and true living cannot exist without it.

It's All Foolosophy

The greatest people to walk this earth were all foolosophers. Here is a list just to mention a few: Albert Einstein, Buddha, Rumi, Mickey Mouse, Mark Twain, Miracle Boy, Lily Tomlin, Lao-Tzu, Bruce Lee, Tracy Ullman, Lucile Ball, The World's Largest Mental Midget, Jonathan Swift, The Beatles, Mike Myers, Dolly Parton, Yoda, Jim Carrey, Jack Nicolson, Merril Streep, Moses, Mother Teresa, Bugs Bunny, all children, and all great moms and dads...

---

4. Shakespeare, A book of quotations, Dover Publications Inc, 1998
5. The Marriage Of Heaven And Hell by William Blake, Dover Publications, 1994

A simple breakdown of foolosophy is: A DAILY PIE IN YOUR FACE, ALAMODE. Foolosophy is the beautiful, spiritual, loving acceptance that you are and have been a fool since birth. And if you are lucky, you will remember this throughout your entire life.

However, most adults forget that they came into this world as fearless, playful, unself-conscious children, eager to make fools of themselves in their daily performances. This is when humor must come into the picture to remind them of their true nature, their original greatness. That is, playful risk-takers, curious, wide-eyed, spontaneous creatures looking to connect and have some fun.

A more complex breakdown of foolosophy, from the bible[6] is: LET NO MAN DECEIVE HIMSELF IF ANY MAN AMONG YOU SEEMITH TO BE WISE IN THIS WORLD, LET HIM BECOME A FOOL THAT HE MAY BE WISE.

---

6. Corinthians, 3:18

Foolosophy Takes the Pressure Off of God.

It is the highest wisdom. The learning, living, and loving never stop. This is because it is humor's task to keep opening and expanding your consciousness throughout time. Thus, putting all time on your side.

Foolosophy is the official fountain of youth. With practice, it will allow you to adopt the inner child/fool persona as characterized by ego-less detachment from ordinary social-emotional controlling patterns and practices. It is a mind game that makes the game of life a blast for all human beings!

PLAY then becomes the four-letter word for life, love, and work. Without the play element, true living ceases to exist and every fool knows it! In foolosophy, the people who can laugh at themselves daily are the most successful human beings of all.

You see, all foolosophers practice the art of laughing at oneself daily because it leads to true self-love. The great Victor Borge stated[7], "The shortest distance between two people is laughter." Therefore, we can infer that the shortest distance between loving yourself, is laughing at yourself. In fact, foolosophy is the greatest love affair a person can have with themselves. And let's be honest, if you cannot truly love yourself, how can you honestly love another?

As children, we lead with our hearts. As we age and our hearts get broken, we begin to lead with our heads. Humor is used to repair and protect this bridge between our heart and our head. So each time it breaks, it can be used as an opportunity to further develop your sense of humor.

A fellow French foolosopher, Francois Truffaut, the famous film critic and director said[8], "When humor can be made to alternate with melancholy, one has a success, but when the same things are funny and melancholic at the same time, it's just wonderful." Humor is your mind viewing the world with a split screen, and the essence of humor lies in the contrast.

---

7. KCET, Victor Borge In Concert
8. Francois Truffaut, brainy quote.com, also see:
http://en.wikipedia.org/wiki/Francois_Truffaut

Humor is the Core of Foolosophy

Humor is the core of foolosophy, the link to our humanity, as well as the key to our sanity. Here are 12 reasons supporting why humor is the most important thing in life and why it should be practiced in everything you do, say, think, feel, and act.

1. It's the #1 sign of human intelligence.
2. It's the key to the future, for it is the best way to view the past.
3. It's the fountain of youth.
4. It makes all people transparent (it gives you x-ray vision)
5. It allows all males to act like "mind readers," which is exactly what every female wants and thinks a man should possess.
6. It's the most important device for all females in dealing with the male ego; the emotional retardation, social ineptness, lack of charm, manners, and childish macho behavior.
7. It's the tool, the device everybody should use to accept personal responsibility for themselves, making personal responsibility healthy, playful, and fun.
8. It reminds people that if they cannot laugh at themselves, they're half dead. Therefore, humor could make them whole again, despite any flaws one may have.
9. It's the best chance at truth and personal freedom. Without truth and personal freedom there is no real love, only superficial, shallow, meaningless, gutless, fear-driven love.
10. It's a shortcut through pain, fear, anger, frustration, and human stupidity.
11. It's the personality's best friend, whether you're rich or poor. If you're rich, everyone wants a piece of you or your money and you will never know or hear the truth. If you're poor, all you can afford is laughter's joy and the solace of believing that "less is more."
12. It's something every truly beloved spiritual person has possessed throughout history, for it is loaded with compassion, respect, and love for all humanity.

I'll stop at a dozen, but remember that with humor in our head, hearts, and souls, we can all be ourselves without fear of what is being said, felt, or shared...

OK, 12 is not enough because the advantages of humor are endless, here is lucky # 13, 14, & 15:

13. It allows all self-expression to flow freely.
14. It tickles one another's brains, like kittens and puppies when they play, and as the signs in my neighborhood so clearly acknowledge, "Children at play"
15. It is flying down the highway in your car singing, screaming, moving, dancing, and gyrating uncontrollably to your favorite tune on the radio.

Chapter 2

Two of the Greatest Foolosophers who Ever Lived...

Charles Dickens and Oscar Wilde:

Mr. Dickens' foolosophy is a major theme of foolosophy: "I feel an earnest and humble desire, and shall till I die, to increase the stock of harmless cheerfulness" (wherever I go)[9].

This has been my foolosophy all my life, and being born and raised in Los Angeles, it has not been an easy ride. No one survives in LA, or I should say, no one can remain a foolosopher for very long without a gigantic sense of humor.

Mr. Wilde stated[10], "Some cause happiness wherever they go, others, whenever they go." This book is for people who wish to transfer pain and misery wherever they go (there would be no point in writing a book for fellow foolosophers). For misery does not need company, it merely needs to be lessened through the eyes of humor. Like great athletes, humor can be used in the following way: When someone tries to dispel misery on you, say to them, "Please do not bring

---

9. Charles Dickens, Public Speech, Edinburgh, June 25, 1841
10. Wit & Wisdom by Oscar Wilde, Dover Publications, 1998

your pain and misery onto my court, onto my field, for I will only reflect it back in your face for being stupid enough to try and dump it on me."[11] Humor makes you fearless, and when you are dealing with negativity of any kind, remain strong, remain brave, put a smile on your face, and rise above.

We are desperate for more and more foolosophers in the world today, so I sure hope this book has a huge impact on you.

---

11. Darrell Ruocco, the Author of this book

Chapter 3
I Couldn't Care More

The Comic Mind

Howard Stern cares, George Carlin cares, Bill Maher cares, John Stewart cares, Chris Rock cares, Roseanne cares, Lily Tomlin cares, Tracy Ulman cares, Lucille Ball cared, Richard Pryor and Bill Hicks (Stand Up comic died at age 33) cared. All great comic minds throughout history cared. It's just that when you use humor to go after the truth it appears you don't care, for you must be fearless in your quest to bring truth forward.

This is how humor and laughter work in your head, heart, and soul. It is the way of the comic mind. So it is very important that you appreciate and understand how the comic mind works, for it is the greatest human mechanism dealing with and coping with the scariest thing of all... how much we can feel, care, and love. This single, lousy, dumb book has almost killed me and it may still yet for it is not quite complete. It has only taken me fifteen years to write because I care so much. Writing it has given me a better appreciation, an understanding, and more love for humor and its endless advantages.

I do appreciate, understand, and even enjoy all the fore mentioned comic minds using my own comic mind to distinguish and separate the good, the bad, and even the ugly things about them, as well as any other human being on the planet. But that is the problem when you see a lot with a large sense of humor; awareness can be a most painful thing. So let me extend my apology and sympathy to you, the reader, if this book causes you any painful awareness. It's okay; it will be a good test for your comic mind.

Chapter 4
I'm Not Kidding

Human beings have gotten too good at lying to one another, too good at lying to themselves, and too good at being lied to. This is not healthy, wise, or loving.

The main reason we are getting so good at lying to one another and everyone else is because of competition. We are competing for men, women, jobs, status; we are even competing on who can be a better liar! However, competition can be healthy and extremely beneficial when used with truth.

I think it was Nietzsche who said, "What doesn't kill you makes you stronger". In foolosophy the new expression is, "What doesn't kill you helps you further develop your appreciation and understanding of humor's true importance." Because the truth is, you may be the only one who knows what the truth is.

Humor allows you to use your imagination, and all foolosophers would agree with Albert Einstein when he said, "Imagination is greater then knowledge". Can't you imagine politicians sitting around drinking their cocktails, smoking cigars, laughing amongst themselves knowing that we the people are screwed? Why do you think great comics make fun of politics and politicians? Answer: Because it eases the pain in knowing the truth about the lies, deception, corruption, that goes on in all man made institutions, bureaucracy, governments, and systems.

Mr. Aldous Huxley said[12], "Ye shall know the truth, and the truth shall make you mad." But who wants to stay in an angry state of consciousness? Humor is all about expanding one's consciousness. An open mind is a receptive mind. The sting of truth might pain you initially, but in your innate ability to smile, even laugh at all truths, you can rise above the pain.

Foolosophers are constantly seeking to open their comic mind in hopes of better seeing the world as a comedy, rather than a tragedy. This is much more fun, and makes life a lot less complicated. Truth brings you out of the dark into the light. So the next time you are in the company of a liar, just remember, people lie for many different reasons; use your sense of humor to seek out the real truth of their intention. Everybody knows the expression the truth shall set you free, but true liberation comes when you can laugh at it.

---

12. The Portable Curmudgeon Redux, by Aldous Huxley, Penguin Group, 1992

Chapter 5

A Smiling Mind

My hope, my wish, my purpose, is to assist you in learning and practicing "the art of laughing at yourself". In my heart and soul, I believe it is the highest art form, even though it is a thinking man's/woman's/child's game.

Children everywhere have a natural sense of humor, which leads to an innate, instinctual, ability to laugh at themselves. This is good news for all adults. The point of foolosophy is simply to remind you of your original greatness.

Nothing on the planet can stand up to a strong sense of play, and a highly imaginative, creative, improvisational sense of humor. This is what we all have and should be used to tap into whatever greatness is in a person while likewise better dealing with the worst in people. *Imagination was given to man to compensate him for what he is not, and a sense of humor was provided to console him for what he is.*[13]

It is your sense of humor and your ability to sincerely honestly laugh at yourself that will better allow you to look at the negative aspects

---

13. Attributed to both Francis Bacon (http://tinyurl.com/2yhgtl) and Oscar Wild (http://www.quotedb.com/quotes/2337)

of your personality. And the quicker you can do this, the sooner you can move back into a positive state of consciousness, and begin to play again. Self-humor and your ability to laugh at yourself is the shortcut to self-love. There is absolutely no way in China you will ever be able to truly love yourself if you cannot cathartically howl at the human errors you have made and will make in your lifetime.

I am a very critical person, I have always beaten up on myself, and this in turn has brought me a lot of mental and emotional pain. But because I did this, it lead me to discover the heart and soul of humor, which is pain. I do recommend beating up on yourself too, and being critical of all your human stupidity. A life without reflection is not worth living. Upon self-reflection, use humor and laughter to make the inner journey less painful.

Emotions rule our lives but humor allows us to be better rulers over our emotions. Real maturity is having the ability to keep a smiling mind at all times to better govern your emotional world. Remember, you are a fool. Humor is the adult toy to play with that will keep us all more socially, emotionally, and mentally playful.

"You can discover more about a person in an hour of play than in a year of conversation."
Pluto... Oh wait... I mean Plato

Chapter 6
Bigger, Badder, Better

"This nation has no sense of humor"
George Carlin

From Clinton & Me, by Mark Katz[14]. Mr. Katz helped Mr. Clinton in better dealing with the "White Water" story as well as developing his sense of humor to better deal with the job of being president of the United States. Mr. Katz relayed the message to President Clinton that:

> Things are only as bad as the stuff you can't joke about. I was eager to play high stakes, and all of my instincts told me that humor's biggest payoff can come at the hour of maximum danger. Maybe on the long list of reasons why "White Water" was not "Watergate" was this guy, the president, could stand up in front of three thousand rapid reporters and show the courage to laugh at the very idea. Self-deprecating humor comes naturally to only the most skillful practitioners of public power. (And your average Jew)

Despite Mr. Clinton's high IQ, and being president of the United States, emotions still ruled a big part of his reasoning abilities, and according to the article, Mr. Clinton was a tad reluctant to become a humorist.

---

14. Clinton & Me by Mark Katz, Miramax Books, 2004

Even politicians are human beings, which is always difficult for me to remember. I don't like politicians. I won't talk politics with anyone, for it is a waste of time and breath.

In humor's view, we have a new preamble to the constitution: "We the people are screwed." If politicians can be bought and sold, and they can never (or rarely) leave their bias, who is really looking out for you and me? If you think your guy is better than the other guy, then you have narrow vision as well, and I am sure your sense of humor desperately needs this book to better assist you in opening your mind, if you don't mind me saying so.

In the article, Mr. Katz uses self-directed humor and made fun of being a Jew. This made me laugh because Jews are my life, I love Jews. But then again, I love blacks, whites, yellows, Mexicans, Muslims, Christians, Buddhists, atheists, realists, pragmatists, Italians, French, Australians, rednecks, no necks...

In this book, and in my life, I am constantly attempting to joke about everything, often exaggerating to make a point, or two, or three. What is most important for you and I is that we cover our own a-- by developing our individual sense of humor to protect ourselves no matter what label is thrust upon us. Learn the art of laughing at oneself for it is up to you and me in our social and emotional political, intercourse, discourse, to cover one another's back because no government, agency, system, or bureaucracy is going to do so. We are all on our own.

The British House of Commons, or parliament, is very fun to watch at work on CSPAN because they are witty and playful in exchanging their thoughts and ideas in comparison to our humorless politicians, caring out their mental masturbation. We should model our system after theirs. And please, I love America, that's why I'm writing the book. So I'm not going to go over there and live in the fog and eat lousy food, even if Tony Blair has a sense of humor and is ten-times more articulate than President Bush.

Chapter 7
Television Through Humor's Vision

Art Imitating Life

Fear sells, conflict sells, drama sells, tragedy sells, misery sells, and pain sells. All great things for you to learn from; however, remembering that pain is the great teacher and humor is the great healer, is key. The best part of television is that it shows you life as if you are experiencing it for yourself. But just like in life, don't take it too seriously. Use humor to laugh at what you see as if you are laughing at yourself.

This book is designed to help you see your life as a comedy, not as a tragedy. Ironically you can develop your appreciation and sense of humor more quickly by watching the bad acting in soap operas for they closely represent the bad acting we experience in real life situations. Men, sit with your girlfriends, wives, and develop your appreciation for humor together. Watching women and men acting emotionally childish, throwing tantrums, throwing dishes, throwing verbal and physical punches is comedic therapy of the highest order.

Life is drama, and by using television as a giant mirror reflecting back to us what we don't want to act like, it reveals our bad habits, bad behavior, and bad acting. Humor is what we have to remove the tension and stress in life. This is why deep down we actually want to laugh when we see someone flying off the emotional charts. Through observing the negative human emotions on television and laughing at them, our brains will not fall trap to imitating this behavior.

This then makes television a good thing, not an abusive thing. When I sit with male friends and acquaintances watching sports of all kinds, we laugh at the anger, rage and insanity, of our testosterone at work. Again, consciously or unconsciously, we are laughing as a form of liberation witnessing the duality of our nature.

All adults should take advantage of television and sit with their kids pointing out all the ugly behavior, bad behavior, seizing this opportunity to talk about the advantages of keeping humor in mind, especially and most importantly when emotions run hot.

For example, when viewing a lousy talk show and people get worked up, leaping out of their chairs, throwing things and yelling obscenities, it is a great opportunity to laugh at their human stupidity to remind you of your own human stupidity. Always view television as if it is a mirror of yourself, because it is.

Television is great because on any channel there is a lesson to be learned about being human. This is the ultimate way to learn from other people's mistakes so that you hopefully will not have to go through the same pain and frustration yourself. Laugh at the mistakes you see on television as if they were your own. This is another great way to develop your sense of humor.

Chapter 8
Love Thy Neighbor

It may not say so in the bible, but in foolosophy we say you cannot love thy neighbor unless you can laugh at thy neighbor. In today's world one's sense of humor is tested constantly. Truthfully, there is no let up.

I've lived in my present home for fifteen years when I decided to do a little home renovation, pretty much a face-lift, which involved painting my house, fixing up the front yard, replacing the grass and surrounding hedges and planting a few flowers. Now, the neighbors directly across the street from me have lived in their house for more then thirty years. They are an older couple seemingly not interested in being "neighborly." I discovered this when they came over with a laundry list of items; things they wanted me to do to my house, to please them.

Where I live has become a pretty affluent, well-maintained community; so when viewing my neighbor's house, it can be perceived as quite the anomaly. It has the original paint, has never been painted, their grass has been dead for years, they have a rusty old boat that has never been moved sitting next to an old car that has perpetually flat tires. It cracked me up that here I am meeting my neighbors for the first time and they're presenting me with their list of things to do to my house. A girlfriend was visiting me at the time and she was in shock while I was smiling and laughing.

All my life, the more ridiculous, stupid, inane, insane things are, the wider my smile becomes. They had eight things listed that they wanted, excuse me, actually demanded that I do, right down to their preferred color choice of paint for my house. When I asked them in a joking manner if this was the extent of their list, or if there would be more items forth coming, they didn't smile apparently not seeing the humor in any of this. My girlfriend started to get really angry and said, "Are you out of your #$#! mind?" The smile continued to lay dormant upon my face as I thanked them for their list, folded it, and asked them if they would also be willing to pay for the cost of these items. Again there was no smile or laughter on their end. And in so many words they pretty much said to me, "Are you out of your #$#! mind?"

Chapter 9
Developing Your Sense of Humor

Your sense of humor is the easiest thing in the world to develop, but you have to be in the world to develop it. This means you have to become more socially emotionally involved with people face-to-face. I know it's a war out there, but there is nothing like hand-to-hand combat, going eyeball-to-eyeball with the multitude of personalities to truly appreciate and understand the necessity of humor in all human, inhuman encounters.

In today's world everyone needs and wants to be constantly entertained. In humor's vision the entertainment never stops, for people are the greatest source of entertainment. You just have to think of it that way. Humor gives us all the perspective to make life a constant source of entertainment. It's live TV where the laughs never stop. Here are 12 ways to develop your sense of humor.

1. *Become the Observation Tower* – You can build your observation tower anywhere you want. This means you can sit in the coffee shop, stand in line at the bank, the super market, anywhere, and just observe human behavior at work. This will give you back your original eyes, the eyes of the child as you remain still and absorb like a little

sponge all adult behavior. This is the foundation for developing your sense of humor. It is something we already do automatically but now you are just going to become more conscious of it.

2. *Find the Lost Art of Story Telling* – Story telling is another form of entertainment and it provides insights and lessons to use in life. You can tell stories over various mediums such as the phone or through emails, but there is nothing like being face-to-face. In doing so, you can study people's body language, their movements, mannerisms, and emotions more closely. This is very important to combat the fact that we are becoming more like the machines we operate on a daily basis, and less like humans. Also in your story telling, please work on telling your most frustrating, exasperating, painful stories in a more humorous way. It's like what you did in high school that comes under the title, "Can you believe this happened to me?" For it is in stories of disbelief of the insanity and pain that you live through that you will eventually get to the laughter that comes through the mere fact of knowing that you lived through the insanity.

3. *Become a Social Butterfly* – Because I began as a shy corpulent (fat) child up to the age of twelve, I'm happy to tell you there is no such thing as an introvert. We all have the desire to be extroverts. Once I found friends and acquaintances that I felt comfortable with, I shed my shy and introverted ways and began making a fool of myself. This is the natural course every child follows. This is precisely why we have humor to move as we make our way to adulthood. Become a social butterfly, spread your wings, and know that the future holds a very high failure rate for you.

4. *Admit You Are an Emotional Retard* – I have a lot of personal experience for I come from a long line of bad communicators, bad listeners, and it really helps that <u>I'm a male, for males have a huge advantage over females when it comes to being emotionally retarded.</u> Don't get me wrong, females need humor just as much as we do, only for different reasons. Emotions will mess up your head and break your heart so much that you will spend many days dazed and confused. You'll end up depressed, but please remember depression is a good thing, for it gives us all a great opportunity to do some soul searching. Strangely enough, it is in your days of hurting and grappling with your emotions that you will make your discovery and find your sense of humor.

5. *Keep Pain and Suffering a Private Affair* – Ladies, I know you like to vent, call your girlfriends, tell your stories of woe, and I want you to keep doing this because story telling is important. However, it is important to sit alone, all by yourself, and ask all the tough questions of yourself, even if you can't find any answers because most of the time there are no answers. This alone should develop your sense of humor. (Men naturally have an advantage of doing their suffering alone, but then again, as many great comics have pointed out, men have lost their cahones and become so hyper-sensitive that they have lost their ability to reason, creating a society of immature childish wimps.)

6. *Act Against Type* – A great actor on stage or on film does not like to be stereotyped, pigeon holed. Humor is the greatest tool for all actors because we actors on the world stage don't like to be stereotyped or labeled either. Besides, we are complex creatures, and as you will discover in this book and in life, identities are the silliest thing of all. If someone is trying to put you in a box smile and take them in a more playful direction where they might really discover who you are.

7. *Watch Television* – Because there's so much to laugh at on Television. You can find endless sources of malfunction, dysfunction, chaos and disturbing news to test yourself. Learn to smile and laugh at the pain you see and feel.

8. *Read Books* – Because watching Television could destroy your brain. We're trying to expand your consciousness not diminish it.

9. *Watch Movies* – Movies are a great source of brilliant people knowledge. All sources of media are a mirror into our heart, soul, and are the keys to Foolosophy.

10. *Talk Foolosophy Wherever You Go* – Especially in your sleep!

11. *Never forget that there's nothing funnier than the truth* – The truth can only set you free if you can honestly, sincerely laugh at it.

12. *Always wear the confident smile of a Foolosopher.*

Chapter 10 Whatever

This is a simple word with huge implications. I have tracked this word for many years. "Whatever" is the subconscious antidote to "Overwhelmed." Many words and expressions are thrown around to describe and/or help us through our growing malaise. If you think this funk is not growing day-by-day, it is only because you do not have time to think.

The purpose of these silly titles, short thoughts, short stories, are to make you think of yourself, think foolosophy, and then think humor as you unlearn what might be holding you back from feeling more, caring more, living more, and generally having more fun. We hear words like, apathetic, desensitized, dehumanized, impersonal, checked out, shut down, tossed around like candy. This prevalent attitude can be most succinctly conveyed with the overused "whatever". We have become a "whatever society".

After attempting to think back upon the first time we as a society heard the word "whatever" used in context, I had a vision of Archie Bunker, the obnoxious, bigoted, close-minded caricature we loved to hate. Archie Bunker's use of "whatever" represented his complete disregard for others and their opinions. We found it hilarious when

Archie would reply, "whatever" any time he wished not to deal with whomever or whatever he was addressing. We are now a society who has collectively become the character we used to laugh at.

Never use the word "whatever". When you hear a friend, acquaintance, anyone, use this word, stop and ask them how long they have been overwhelmed, and what it is exactly they wish not to deal with. If it is you with whom they do not want to deal, resolve it right then and there. "Whatever" is for a spoil sport, a childish baby who says, "Screw it...I don't want to play, I don't want to deal. I don't care."

Take a stand in fighting this disease. If you want to have more meaning and fun in life, please eliminate this vile, repugnant, aggravating, stupidest of all words. The biggest threat and/or scare are not guns, knives, bombs, WMDs, earthquakes, fires, hurricanes; it is the state of apathy.

To counteract this, we must play like big kids. We must throw ideas, feelings, and words around like balls of play. Keep throwing and catching with your sense of play and the game of life is sweet. By the simple act of playing, you are showing you care.

Part II
To Be or Not to Be: Spiritual!

God made laughter good and healthy, and then gave us nothing to laugh at except one another and yourself! It has been said that a child's laughter is the shortest prayer to God; we are all spiritual beings from the get-go, so humor says to just let-go!

Humor reminds us of our original greatness, to be under the influence of humor is a Heavenly state of consciousness.

Chapter 1

Dalai of the West

Hello Dalai! Can you imagine if the Dalai of the East had to live here in LA, go to some job he hated, spend two hours a day trapped in a car on the 405 freeway, then come home to screaming kids starving for food, attention, love? He might not be wearing that little smile he is best known for.

The most spiritually evolved person I have ever met is me. This might make you laugh because LA/Hollywood is joked about as being the most superficial, shallow place on Earth.

In stressing spiritual maturation, please remember that real maturity is possessing the ability to laugh at yourself, including all descriptions and depictions of your personality. Come and live in a world where it does not matter what another human being says about you, where you will not be offended or take it personally. Tongue-in-cheek, I proclaim myself the Dalai Lama of the West-Side of LA, maybe the United States of America, for I have always been able to smile and laugh at all peoples' perceptions of me, as well as my own.

This is because I long ago accepted my God given role as a playful, fun seeking, fool. Again, I am not joking with you, for if you cannot honestly laugh at yourself on your way to knowing who you are, what you are, and what you are all about, you are going to have a lot less fun, and a lot more misery.

This is important so please allow me to explain some of the reasons why:

First, when people cannot get to you, put you down by labeling you, or name calling, it affects them immediately. And if they choose to think about it, reflect on it later in the day, they will be reminded of how foolish they looked earlier in their small attempt.

Second, this means that all human encounters are a source of entertainment for you, and even "pointless diversions" have significance, for you are always learning more and more about the ever-changing human nature.

Third, and most important, is to remember that the fool standing before you is just a mirror to look into, which is a reflection of yourself. Meaning that if you do not like what you see in another person, smile, for that character might be lurking somewhere inside your persona.

Chapter

2 Speak for Yourself

Do not be afraid of expressing what is in your heart, head or soul, for a person with a well developed sense of humor can handle and deal with anything and everything that you have a passion or desire to communicate. All you need now is the mental maturity to use your own sense of humor while all other people express their thoughts, feelings, and opinions to you.

Humor is it. And it is the only thing you have to keep in mind during social emotional mental intercourse. You may be smiling, laughing, at this because you know there is some truth or a lot of truth in what you just read. Or, you're probably smiling, laughing, because you know very few people who have the good sense, the sensibility, and the sensitivity that they are a big part of humor's true nature. These things are not discussed or talked about, just like the compassion, empathy, and forgiveness that's a big part of humor's range as well.

In the eternal struggle to appreciate, understand, and really listen, always keep a smiling mind. Think with humor, talk with humor, and please, share this book with all your friends and acquaintances and talk about the subject of humor and its importance in our lives.

Hundreds of articles and hundreds of books have been written and are being written alerting us to the truths that human beings are becoming more neurotic, more psychotic, ruder, angry, impolite, frustrated, and we all know the diabolical effects of political correctness. It is up to you and me to take back our hearts, souls, and minds as well as our city streets and communities.

Chapter 3

Email from Jesus

Today I got an email from Jesus and I don't even have a computer:

> To the Biggest Fool,
>
> More recently I've noticed you've been taking yourself and the world around you too seriously. Don't follow in my footsteps. Don't crucify yourself because you too have something beautiful to deliver to the world. I know how long it has taken you but keep going, hang in there, don't lose your dynamic sense of humor. I only wish your book was around when I was walking the Earth spreading my beauty. Can you believe that my Dad gave humor and laughter to human beings and I lost the art of laughing at myself? This is what happens to a person when they see how beautiful something is and can't wait to share the beauty with the world, whenever humor is not present. I should have taken my own advice from my book when I said to Mark, "Truly I say to you whoever does not receive the kingdom of God like a child will not enter it at all." And of course I agree with you when you say that all children are born with an innate sense of humor and the gift of laughter. For without

these gifts, moving forward and evolving becomes too difficult and painful. My father was onto something when he gave the world these gifts.

Sincerely

Good Luck

Best of Wishes

Jesus

Chapter 4

I'm Tired of Being Angry...

These words, this thought, came from Oprah Winfrey regarding her pain, frustration, concern about present day society. Oprah knows pain and she knows the value of humor even if she rarely ever talks about it in depth. Pain is tiring, it fatigues your entire being, and it exhausts us all. Because Oprah is so well known, I use her words, for when she takes off her emotional wardrobe, we can identify with her.

Something that is rarely talked about is Oprah's sense of humor. Oprah is not a comedian but she makes us smile, laugh, cry, feel, and think. You can observe her beautiful mind and personality at work whether you are a woman or a man. She will move from tears to laughter after she makes a serious point about something painful. You can actually feel her dissolve, then evolve, in the course of a show.

I rarely watch her show, but I fully appreciate her love, wisdom, wit, and intelligence. A black woman, a fat woman, a thin woman, a woman that knows pain of molestation, abuse, misuse, it is Oprah's understanding of humor that no one talks enough about that draws me to her and I believe helps draw millions of people to her on an unconscious level.

There is nothing funny about abuse, but we are all abused and misused in some way. Watching Oprah's strength of character, as well as being a larger-than-life character, is inspiring. And may I be the first to say it, she is a giant fool that daily takes risks, chances on all stages, and knows the role of being an underdog, a failure, on her way to being lady "O".

Young at heart, young in mind, she helps us all become aware, and she makes our awareness less painful and more beneficial. I would say to her when it comes to anger management, tap into the influences of humor, for they are all around us and in us all if we can only become more aware of their true importance. For in the end, pain is a great teacher and humor is a great healer. Emotional chaos and pain remembered in tranquility upon reflection is how we better develop our sense of humor.

Chapter 5
Angry Soul

O to a Higher Power

It is funny that the day after I wrote, "I'm so tired of being angry..." I picked up the Sunday paper and on the cover of the Calendar section[15] were nine pictures of a smiling Oprah titled, "O to a Higher Power." What is even funnier is that there were thirteen identities, personality traits that they referred to her as, in the article: Activist, Brand, Philanthropist, Mogul, Trend Maker, Experimenter, Producer, Frequent Flyer, Impresario, Enthusiast, Benefactor, Cover Girl, and Confidante. What is even funnier than that is there is still no mention of the power of her sense of humor.

Yet what is even funnier than that is, that juxtaposed beside the Oprah article is an article on Howard Stern, another angry soul who knows and uses humor to make millions of people laugh. However, I don't get the impression that he is truly happy with himself or life in general, whereas I believe Oprah uses humor everyday to push through her pain and anger. The way I see it is that Oprah loves herself for the gold that resides inside her, where Howard hasn't yet made the personal leap to truly loving himself.

---

15. Sunday edition LA Times Calendar section, 2006

Two different characters, two of our most well known celebrities, and the difference I feel is the spiritual aspect of humor in one's heart, soul, and mind. This is the spiritual paradigm that Oprah exudes. THIS IS WHAT WE ALL HAVE TO WATCH FOR IN THE PEOPLE WE ADMIRE AND LOOK UP TO.

Life is about finding your own inner-strength by using your own sense of humor to evolve and move through your anger and pain to become a more spiritual being. Perhaps Howard is being held back by his ego and intellect. He makes fun of himself daily, he makes a fool of himself and a fool of everyone else on the radio, but at the end of the day I believe he holds onto his anger and pain because he fears letting go of his ego and intellect. After all, they are what made him famous.

I'm attempting to point out what I believe is to be the spiritual aspect of humor that all of us desire and need to move toward self-love. I feel this is a huge difference between Oprah and Howard. This could be the most important point of the book, so let me bring in a third character, a man who died the day before this article came out, who was the best at using humor to make us laugh… Richard Pryor.

It was well known that Mr. Pryor was not that happy a man in life. He was indeed an angry soul, apparently unable to turn his humor inward to liberate himself from his own darkness. This has always been the big question of the comic mind. And in trying to differentiate the contrast between Oprah's use of humor and Mr. Stern's / Mr. Pryor's use of humor, hopefully you too will be able to see it in your own life.

This is my interpretation for I have no personal facts beyond the power of observation of these characters through the medium of TV, radio, and an occasional article in the newspaper. None of us will ever know the truth of what is in the heart and soul of Oprah, Howard Stern, or Richard Pryor, all we can ever do is use the humor in our own heart and soul to help liberate us from our negative emotions, thoughts, and feelings. The reason I know this so well is I've kept just enough anger and pain in my own heart and soul to attempt to deliver this book to the world.

Chapter 6
Pure Silliness

Pure silliness is the ultimate physical and mental state of being. It is the most divine, euphoric, sublime, spiritual place, and no one talks about it at length, and few experience it after a certain age. Being in a state of pure silliness almost daily allows highly evolved people to think I am highly evolved too. However, pure silliness feels more like highly dissolved.

In the dictionary, evolve does not explain silliness; dissolve comes the closest to defining it. You feel like you are liquid dispersed everywhere and nowhere. You disappear for minutes at a time (or longer in my case). My silliness comes from my awareness of the paradox, irony, and appreciation of the foolishness of every moment. It comes from the contradiction and contrast of every thought, whether it be my own, or of the person standing before me.

The differences I see when viewing the same situations and acts throughout the day, knowing all this and yet knowing nothing at all, lead to a profound trust of everyone and everything. Trust is the most important ingredient in achieving pure silliness, for you are the most open and vulnerable when you do, yet no one can see it; it being the utter joy that comes from the state of silliness. In this state, you love everything and everyone.

When I leave this state of pure silliness, I am sad for a moment, then, like all great events, I want to share the experience. Like a great meal, I want everyone to go to the restaurant. I want to see their faces as they taste it, and make those expressions of ecstasy and sounds of an infant. Unfortunately, I can only write about my silliness in hope that others, as they read this, can remember their own moments of silliness, and somehow, with this book, resurrect the most important elements innately possessed by us all. That is, trust, awareness, and vulnerability. It is only when you learn to trust yourself, sharpen your awareness of others, and increase your tolerance for vulnerability, that you can achieve this ultimate state of being...the state of pure silliness.

Part III
Beautiful Cripple

Fear is the absence of humor; so says my radio & writing partner Jon Dubin (Patient Zero). Humor is the lighthouse that shines a floodlight that exposes our duality. This allows us to more quickly move out of the darkness and into the light; this is humor's true essence and beauty.

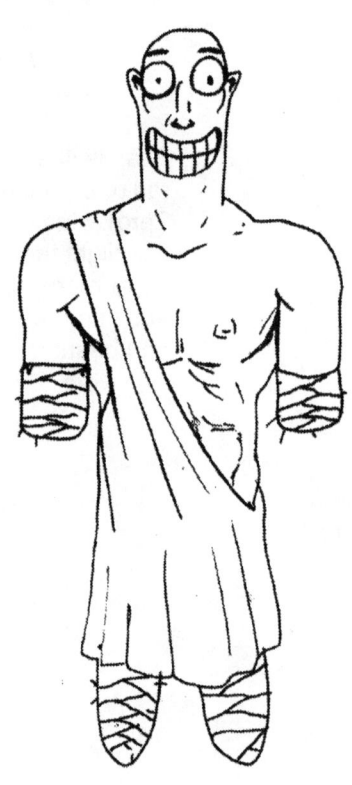

Chapter 1

Beautiful Cripple

Only in humor's vision can we have any real equality for we are all unequal, and this is where the laughter comes into play. Every person you will encounter in this lifetime is flawed and handicapped in some or many ways.

This truth should allow you to smile in complete confidence. Most people attempt to hide their flaws. But this is like wearing a bad toupee. You're fooling no one but yourself. But please, be my guest, for it would be no fun and there would be much fewer laughs if we didn't attempt to conceal our imperfections.

Thank God we were made different because this would be most mind-numbing if we were not. Humor allows us to develop a good and healthy perceptive, an auxiliary tool for our judgments. Now we must learn to suspend our judgment long enough to give perception a better chance. This might be difficult in the beginning but the rewards are huge. Humor is the universal gift that gives us the objectivity, elasticity, and flexibility in our own individual personality to not only tolerate and withstand, but also enjoy all human differences. Humor says enjoy the hunt for the differences that make a difference. Different is good, healthy, fun, laughable. It's about time we enjoy and celebrate our differences.

You can only continue to grow by coming face to face with your inevitable, defects, deficits, and flaws in your own personality. This is the self-understanding of humor. And in laughing at yourself you can transcend whatever personality type you are. Now how much fun is that? Real maturity is laughing at oneself, for there is nothing funnier than your immediate perception of yourself, because that perception will change in time.

This is why humor puts all time on your side. For as you change and grow and evolve over the years, humor makes all traveling a much more pleasurable, healthy, fun experience. No matter what personality type you think you are, never forget you are first and for most a beautiful fool. Laughing at anything that is negative in your personality will immediately move you into a more positive state of consciousness. This is the theme and the thrust of foolosophy.

Chapter 2
The Art of Teasing

As a male, teasing is one form of humor that I absolutely love and value. To have any real fun, I believe teasing and being teased are an absolute must.

Men seem to have an advantage, or at least a head start, when it comes to teasing. In sports, guys tease one another all the time. It is a form of affection and an acknowledgement of an underlying bond. Here is a generalization about male athletes and the topic of hair:

If any male, a grown man or a young boy, gets a funky or different kind of haircut, his teammates will say upon seeing his new hairdo, "Nice cut, did you lose a bet?" or "That must be the cut you get to drive women away!" Or if a teammate happens to be wearing a hat, he will simply hand it to him and say something like, "Please, do us all a favor, put this on your head and don't take it off until your hair grows out!" What a friend! Now, as little boys and big boys, we often forget that this form of humor is best appreciated by our own sex, and it would be a mistake to engage in this form of teasing with the women in our lives, or an women in general.

Imagine a girlfriend or wife coming home after 3 or 4 hours of primping at the hair salon, only to have the man in her life, who happens to be sitting around with the boys drinking beer and watching football, greet her as she comes in the door with a big smile and the remark, "Here honey, you can wear my hat until it grows out."

No man in his right mind would dare say or do something of the sort (although many might think it). If they are smart, they have learned that women will not respond to teasing in the same manner another man would. She will not likely laugh, reciprocate in the banter, or come back at a later time with an appropriate means of retaliation also by means of teasing. Most likely, she will be hurt, angry, or both.

Since man has always been and will always be chasing woman, this game can be made more fun, interesting, and understandable for women if they became more familiar with, "The Art of Teasing". It can be referred to as an "art form" because it is a skill or knack men have developed in order to laugh at our many defects. Females would gain a great advantage from learning this art form so that we, as men, can no longer accidentally or intentionally put them on the defensive, making them insecure, shy, and constantly second guessing themselves.

When not armed with the freedom to tease, men have to resort back to that annoying behavior of a quick perfunctory remark, and then an equally quick retreat back to the game on television, the newspaper, or any other activity in which we can quickly engage ourselves so as to not address the uncomfortable situation at hand. In a strange convoluted way, teasing allows men to tell the truth in the least hurtful way. In other words, it is not intended to put down, but rather, to tell the other person we are on the same team and that we enjoy each others' company.

In the military, in sports, and especially in the business world, teasing is a way to expedite the expression of thoughts and feelings because men in general are so often completely inept at expressing themselves in any other way. To put it simply, it is just how we're built.

Chapter 3 Between the Ears

**Mature /
Immature**

You grow up the day you have your first real laugh at yourself. Real maturity is having the ability to smile, laugh at oneself.

Men, if you think you are a real man, and you want to keep it real, be real, be cool, stay cool, maintain and impress the ladies, than humor and foolosophy are for you. By using humor you are being cooler than cool to maintain your cool. I'm laughing at myself right now because in my daily speak I don't use the word cool or the expression "keep it real."

This is what we mean when we say it requires much more strength to pull (hold) the punch then throw it. The same holds true for harsh thoughts and words. Humor is what we all have for our emotional, social maturity, which in time gives you the mental maturity to deal with everything and everyone. And if you think you cannot laugh at yourself, then you haven't taken a good hard look.

"It should be borne in mind that although my heart was breaking I could still enjoy a good laugh. It was this ability to laugh in spite of everything that saved me. I had already known that famous line from Rabelias, 'for all yours ills, I give you laughter.' I can say from personal experience that it is a piece of the highest wisdom. There is so precious little of it today – it's no wonder the drug pushers and the psycho analysts are in the saddle." This quote is from the great foolosopher Henry Miller[16].

From Mahatma Gandhi[17], *"If I had no sense of humor, I would long ago have committed suicide."* Humor is a lifesaver.

A friend of mine said, "Humor is the lubricant which allows the human mind to expand more smoothly."

The men mentioned above are not stand up comics; they are intelligent sensitive compassionate men that I know who took the time to develop their appreciation and understanding of humor. Truly, you are only in competition with yourself, and instead of running away from you childish, small-minded behavior, instead of running away from your anger and fears, practice using humor to face your worst enemy, YOU!

---

16. Nothing But The Marvelous: Wisdoms of Henry Miller by Henry Miller, Capra Press, 1999
17. Mahatma Gandhi, Gandhiserve.org

Why not have some laughs kicking your own butt, making self-discovery, self-awareness, less painful, and a lot more fun. No male escapes being a jerk, a dick, or a small-minded twerp". There is an endless list of names for men at their immature worst, and humor will not only help us endure them all, but it will also help us face them all, then escape them all after we do our mirror time.

Yes, you must practice daily in the mirror, reliving, reviewing all negative names hurled your way, as well as being creative, improvisational, making up your own personal favorites for your daily dumb-jerk moves.

At first, you may drop your head while staring in the mirror in disgust, get angry, get frustrated, growl at yourself in the mirror, beat up on yourself for being a moronic jerk, but keep standing there until it sinks in. I promise you will crack a smile, lift your new improved head up, and begin a new day with a good hard belly laugh at the old you.

Real maturity is personal freedom between the ears where the big boys play. In sports, in dating, in business, in marriage, in life, we are eternally involved in the game between the ears. Instinctually we all know humor's true value in becoming a man. To attempt to fool, or deceive the man in the mirror, is foolish and immature. To laugh at the man in the mirror with sincerity and conviction is using humor as the personality's best friend.

Why? Because the truth will set you free when you can honestly laugh at it. As Oscar Wilde said[18], "A friend is someone who will stab you in the chest." So be a friend to yourself, go to the kitchen, pull out your sharpest longest knife, and bleed for all the right reasons. Remember, I never learned anything from being right, only from being wrong, thick headed and stupid. As males we can grow in direct proportion to our ability to honestly laugh at our narrow-minded thinking and acting.

Humor's development is a tricky business when starting out. This is why foolosophy says, "Take everything as a compliment". With this mindset, you may filter out negative criticism from positive or constructive criticism later, upon reflection. Humor is the minds "check and balance" system where you keep the books so no one can cheat you.

---

18. Wit and Wisdom by Oscar Wilde, Dover Publications, 1998

Remember, no one can put you down but you, and by putting yourself down with humor long enough to objectively look, you will only heighten your perspective on the rebound.

If you have, or have had critical teachers, coaches, and parents in your life, do not be crushed by their criticism. Begin using your sense of humor to decipher what is false and what is true in developing your personality as you grow. Humor is always searching for the truth; you'll instinctively know what to hold onto and what to throw away.

Chapter

4 Humor's Balance

Perhaps you have heard the expression, "Everything in moderation". With this in mind, you will not develop your appreciation or understanding of what humor is for. Remember, the essence of humor is contrast. The good news is most kids, teenagers, college students, and adults as well, already know extreme behavior. For we have all watched extreme behavior on television, sitting in our living rooms, laughing at the insanity we see.

Twenty-five centuries ago, Plato observed that imitation of human behavior soon ceases to be imitation and tends to become reality for the imitator. Kids imitate what they see, adults imitate what they see. This is a universal truth, and there is nothing funnier than an expert on TV telling us that TV does not affect us. This is like the panel of experts on television who originally told the nation, the world, that there was nothing harmful in cigarettes.

The other night my friend Russell came over and asked me to turn on a television show called, "The Biggest Loser", where really heavy, large fat people lose weight in yet another form of competitive extremes. I felt a full range of emotions watching people who once weighed 300-400 pounds cry and laugh, laugh and cry, as they stepped on and off a giant scale showing the world how much weight they have knocked off.

Television represents extreme human behavior and although it leans heavily towards extreme stupidity, I still love it. Like everything else in life, television is best viewed using one's sense of humor to filter out the crap, from the greatness that it has to offer. Lots of funny things are revealed on TV that is not always under the heading of comedy. Through it we view a world of contrast, contradictions, and conflict.

I'm writing this book exemplifying, exaggerating the point of contrast, because extreme behavior is total contrast. This makes it naturally funny. We might watch a very fat person on television and burst out laughing, but we know in life the emotional, social, mental implications, and spiritual pain that could be attached to being overweight. Nonetheless, I know lots of people who are overweight, fat, and have a tremendous sense of humor about themselves and their extreme eating. The same can be said about my friends who are extreme athletes, extreme TV viewers, and extreme freaks, geeks, and knuckleheads. But all of these people have the same thing in common, they are happy, they know humor, they live a life of contrast.

If you are an extreme person with extreme tendencies, please use your sense of humor for it will only help you balance this behavior. At the end of the day, however, all people should be under the influence of humor no matter who they are, how they live, what they are viewing, or who's viewing them. It will keep them balanced mentally, and fill them with joy.

Chapter 5
Humor's Intervention

Good habits are just as hard to break as bad habits...

Finding joy in your misery is another way of describing humor, so says my friend Matt. Your life and personality are pretty much the product of your daily habits, and habits repeated day after day become automatic. Start the good habit of laughing at your bad habits.

Foolosophy wants you to look at your life as a comedy. If you cannot change your bad habits, then the next best thing is to laugh at them. Once you get in the habit of laughing at what makes you miserable, you develop and continue developing the powerful habit we call humor.

My friend Matt bites his finger nails, bites his lip, likes to pick his nose, and claims he needs to pick his pimples. In fact, he is so talented that he can often perform all these bad habits at the same time; a true symphony of bad habits that I love to mirror back at him when he performs this rather unattractive behavior. This causes him to chuckle, I chuckle, then there's a bit of momentary anger from Matt to which I laugh a little louder, which in turn makes him laugh again. Then we both end up really laughing hard together.

What is funny about this is Matt is not six-years-old; he is twenty-six-years-old. He says he wants to truly stop this neurotic behavior, so he gave me permission to mock him, to make fun of his bad acting. Laughing at oneself is a good start to knocking off a bad habit or two, for it is just as easy to form a good healthy habit, as it is a bad one. And it is just as difficult to break a good habit, as it is a bad one. Get into the habit of laughing at yourself.

My brother still smokes, he is not going to stop, and everyday he feels awful about it. But because we can both laugh at his continuing to smoke he does not suffer from heavy guilt as well. Every human being is an addict of some sort, we all have bad habits and we all have good habits. When it comes to shedding any habit, laughing at it is the best start.

So, if necessity is the mother of invention, then humor is the father of intervention. The really good quality we human beings have is we can always learn something new once we see a necessity for learning it. Humor knows that we are all beautiful cripples. The beauty of humor and laughing at ourselves means we do not have to give into those handicaps. Truthfully most of the greatest people that walked and crawled this Earth put

forth an unusual effort along the line of their deficiency compensating for their weak points making them their strong points.

Kay Redfield Jamison, in her book Touched with Fire[19], described the great poet Lord Byron as a man of tumultuous passions, fiery and high-spirited, and also as being very moody and melancholy. A study in contrast, his friends observed that his very defects were among the elements of his greatness, and it was out of the struggle between the good and evil principles of his nature that his mighty genius drew his strength.

---

19. Touched with Fire by Kay Redfield Jamison, Free press paperbacks a division of Simon and Schuster Inc., 1993

Chapter 6
There's Definitely Something Wrong With Me

My arms are too long for my body, my nose is too long for my face, my feet are too big to find shoes that fit me, and a lifetime of sports has left me handicapped and reduced to writing this book about how we can all return to the state of play and humor that has drained out of our collective emotional bloodstreams.

In the culture of foolosophy, all our shortcomings, flaws, foibles, individual defects, can become assets. To laugh at ourselves as others laugh at us is to celebrate our humanness; to become ourselves while we help to lift our fellow fools out of their own misery quicksand.

Humor is man's best friend, and our personality's pen pal. The truth not only sets you free, but it makes life a lot more playful, fun, and worthwhile to participate in. Our individuality is born out of humor.

The sliding scale of humor (hilarious to tragic) is a slippery slope of contrasts. Our own unique flaws and shortcomings are the first line of defense against taking everything so damned personally! Foolosophy stares at the full-length mirror that life holds up for us each day, and then explodes with laughter at the reflection staring back. It is nothing less than us accepting us, which opens the way for us accepting another's point of view about us. Stop taking it all so personally, and start taking it like the fool that you are – with a lot of play, fun and humor.

Part IV
I Like My Pain Straight

Humor is the thing that allows us to best relate to one another. We can all sympathize with each other through our collective stories of pain and frustration, which then fosters empathy towards others.

This step to empathy helps us to reach a state of self-realization and sudden awareness without all of the messy pain. FOOLOSOPHY encourages us to share our selfishness about our pain; to go into the personal agony in order to find out who you really are after all. When we watch comedies and laugh at all the dysfunctional characters, we are really laughing at various parts of ourselves; you can use humor in your personal sit-com or home movie in order to feel more comfortable in your own skin.

Chapter 1

Does My Smile Confuse You?

Does My Smile Confuse You, Too?

The Story of Pain	The Story of Humor
Pain is the price we pay for feeling, for playing hard in life, seeking our pleasures, treasures, fun, and the joy in living large. Pain is insane. End of the story.	Humor is what we human beings have to face our pain, tell our stories of pain, better enabling us to remain sane. End of the story.

How you deal with your pain will determine how much fun, joy, love, and laughter you will have in your life. And I have had the good fortune to be immersed in mental, physical, spiritual, and emotional pain, everyday of my life.

Pain is the best teacher, and humor is the great healer. Only an insane person would attempt to teach everyone in the world the joy, freedom, and pleasure in learning the art of laughing at themselves. But I have been called much worse than insane.

Besides, I agree with G.K. Chesterton[20] that "The madman is not the man who has lost his reason, the madman is the man who has lost everything except his reason," and most importantly, his sense of humor. Because my biggest fear is the day I lose my sense of humor, which can only lead me to conclude that reason is not far behind.

Call me crazy, call me insane, call me whatever you want, for I have been labeled, perceived, every which way a human being can be perceived. And all the name calling only puts a bigger smile on my face.

When it comes to the blame game, humor knows that you are responsible for you. So the real joy and fun you can derive in developing a sense of humor will in turn make personal responsibility a healthy, wise thing. Humor makes winners out of losers, and let's be honest, we all feel like losers most of the time, if not all of the time.

You might be thinking "Hey pal, speak for yourself". Well, you bring up a good point, because the best part about humor is that we can all speak for ourselves, remembering this is the land of the free, home of the brave. Humor makes us fearless warriors, where each man and woman is called upon to show the maturity to be able to listen, really listen, to one another without being offended.

If humor cannot open your eyes, open your ears, open all your senses, then it is pretty much over for you. Foolosophy uses humor to remind us all of our original status; the beautiful child. Does any boy or girl really grow up? Foolosophy says no. There are only two kinds of people when it comes to status: childlike and childish. Here is a list explaining each:

---

20. G.K. Chesterton, Quote from the American Chesterton Society Website: http://chesterton.org/discover/lectures/56poetlunatics.html

Childlike:	Childish:
• Playful • Creative • Spontaneous • Wide-eyed • Improvisational • Hungry to Learn • Curious • Fearless • A Natural Actor • A Foolosopher	• Petty • Spoil Sport • Narrow Minded • Scared Stupid • Lost Sense of Play • No Sense of Humor • Puts Down Others To Feel Important • No Fun, Except to Laugh At • Hasn't Read This Book • Doesn't Care

Before 9/11 we were becoming a more serious, un-playful, un-fun, unloving society in general. After 9/11, it has become even worse and fear is dominating our culture. Do not take my word for it, just look to your left or right at the people you pass on the street, really look at the expression they are wearing, and you will have a better understanding of why I am smiling.

"The optimist thinks that this is the best of all possible worlds -- the pessimist fears it is true." – Robert Oppenheimer[21]

Try saying hello to twenty strangers a day as you pass by and mentally record their reactions, their responses. I do this daily in my hood, and most people look down at the ground, or look away. Some even give me confused, perplexed, bewildered, pained expression, for apparently a friendly face, and hello from a stranger has become shocking and scary.

---

21. Robert Oppenheimer, Brightquotes, also see: http://en.wikipedia.org/wiki/Robert_Oppenheimer

One of my most enjoyable responses after saying hello to a stranger in the street is when the person turns around, looking away from my glance, and then turns back at me saying "Are you talking to me? Do I know you?" To which my smile broadens and I reply, "You do now".

Chapter 2
I'm Dead Serious

We are socially emotionally retarded. Social and emotional retardation is our future unless we adopt and adapt humor's wisdom and intelligence.

I have witnessed the human shutdown. Most of the people I attempt to interact with, play with in the course of the day, are too busy playing with their equipment or talking about their equipment to notice that I am playing with them. And when they are not playing with or talking about their equipment, they are too checked out of being human to respond. Perhaps you have noticed the hundreds of thousands of people walking around in a semi-coma. It is not only fear that is shutting them down, but they are getting better and better at operating their equipment and worse and worse at being human.

I am writing this at my local coffee shop hoping against hope to have some great face-to-face, social emotional, mental intercourse, discourse, when I look out the window and begin (nervously) laughing out loud at what I see. A big blue bus is stopped at the signal and everyone on it is plugged into some piece of equipment, or wearing some piece of equipment, staring straight ahead. Then I look around the coffee shop, and seated all around me are lap-toppers and cell phone users. And every other person who enters the coffee shop is either on their cell phone or checking their cell phone, and its only 7:00am!

I am probably the last person in Los Angeles who does not have a cell phone. This is mostly because I am protesting the essay I am writing at present. I also write longhand, so I am not using a laptop. And if I see another human being remotely interested in face-to-face communication, I will gladly, happily put down my pen, so I can practice the most important dying art form, being a human being.

Henri Bergson and George Meredith stated in their book Comedy[22], "What is alive lives by inward discoveries and intensities, not in the external world regulated by clock and calendar. What is alive is not mechanical. What is mechanical suffers a death of the heart."

Humor is always and forever trying to shine a light on things we might need to look at, pay a little more, or a lot more attention to. It is time we look at the big picture in our society, honestly, and use our collective sense of humor, to return back to being human. Humor is the link to our humanity, and the key to our sanity.

Mind, body, spirit, heart, soul, personality, all operate better when we use humor to preserve and protect what makes us all great. Mr. Bergson and Mr. Meredith refer to the comic spirit as the ultimate civilizer in a dull and insensitive world. Humor makes us fearless to look with critical eyes at everything that might hold us back from being bigger badder (meaning greater) better human beings tomorrow.

Using humor in a constructive way, not a destructive way is what foolosophy is all about. It is about a larger perspective and more objectivity. It gives our personality more flexibility and elasticity, like yoga for our minds, which keeps the heart and spirit pumping.

Think of your comic spirit as the childlike spirit resurrected in you, for in each honest sincere laugh you have at yourself, you are reborn again and again. We must imitate life (growth), not death (destruction). The essense of humor is contrast. So take what is deadening to your heart and soul and laugh your way back to life and liberation.

---

22. Comedy, by Henri Bergson and George Meredith, Wylie Sypher, 1956

Chapter 3
Your Royal Insignificance

The road to greatness is filled with greatness. I tried being great for an entire day, it was exhausting. People were lined up outside my door, eager to pick my brain, suck the juice, the life right out of me. So I quickly learned to play myself down, play small, quickly becoming the biggest fool in Los Angeles, which is really saying something, for fools dominate the landscape.

Here is something I did right as a teenager of 16, and a natural athlete: When big-time pain and suffering entered my heart, soul, and psyche, I sat alone with it and let it overwhelm me. At first, I got angry at the pain and suffering, yelled at God, and cried all alone. Then, after some time, I got intimate with the pain and the giant frustration of having two bad knees, and a chronic, dislocating, separating shoulder. Not long after that, I was able to convert my tears of pain and the new reality that I was destined to live with, into humor. I began to view the world with a split screen. And before my 18th birthday, I had uncovered the true value of keeping humor in mind.

Here is one more thing I did right as an athlete, as a human being: I did not go around transferring my pain, anger, and frustration to anyone else. I did what athletes know they have to do, I sucked it up. Pain and suffering are a private affair. Everybody has some kind of pain, and there is nothing funny about the pain that is doled out to any of us. My pain is mine alone, so please, keep your pain to yourself. Use your sense of humor to be worthy of it. Eventually you'll be able to laugh at it and lighten your load.

Chapter 4
Mom's Pain / My Pain

My beloved mother was the first person I laughed with, laughed at. In the human comedy/drama, the mother is the most powerful character, and ironically, paradoxically, the person you and I have to laugh loudest and longest at.

For twenty years or so, my most magnificent highly emotional mom, told me that I would never understand a mother's love. Mom was right, mothers are always right, and I early on surrendered to my caring loving mother by simply smiling at the truth that this child, nor any other child on Earth, would ever be able to fully appreciate or understand a mother's love.

Love itself is the most perplexing, complicated thing on Earth. This only makes humor and laughter more important in simplifying it to keep it alive and well. Here is the funny ironic part: mom did not appreciate or understand my love for her. When she got a worried, pained, fearful expression on her face, I would mock, mimic, imitate her back, mildly upsetting her for a time because grown-ups never want to be made fun of when they are trying to be serious.

As children, we do not understand our mother's over-the-top emotional bad acting and hate to see them like this. So when mom would attempt it, I mirrored back at her as best I could, her pained facial expression to show her how funny she looked. My younger brother Ron is a natural mime and he could do mom's face, voice, body language, mannerisms, perfectly. He was so good that one day mom eventually and inevitably gave in, and from then on we always ended up in loving, hysterical laughing.

What I learned about mom and people in general, myself included, is this: <u>If you have love, real love in your heart, it is real hard to not enjoy being made fun of for all the right reasons.</u> Emotions rule mother's lives. Emotions rule children, people's lives. I know of nothing better than humor to help us all be better rulers over our own emotions. Humor and laughter dominate all negative emotions allowing us to get closer and closer as human beings.

"Humor is the rainbow over suffering..." – Anne R. Colton[23]

---

23. Shorthand Of The Soul: the quotable horoscope by David Hayward, Flare Publications, 1999

Chapter 5
Dad's Anger

As a small child, watching my dad watching a boxing match was the funniest thing because he would stick his chin way out, snarl his lip, grind his teeth, and grunt and grown at the television. He would sit way forward on the couch and I would sit way back on the couch and stare at him. Dad's mean angry face was the scariest face I had ever seen.

Things that scare us are funny. If you don't believe me just watch people in a theater during a scary movie, after a big scare comes nervous laughter to ease the tension. This I learned is our subconscious way of protecting our conscious mind. Nervous laughter is part of the foundation of humor development.

Dad was not very pleased when he one day discovered me and Ron making fun of his mean face in our bedroom, once again reemphasizing the fact that adults do not like to be mocked, made fun of. But eventually, inevitably, dad gave in and laughed. To parents, grown-ups everywhere, children can get nervous, confused, bewildered, in trying to understand adults. Please remember this and dig deeper into your own memories of childhood.

Practice making your own angry faces in the mirror in a kind of self-mockery, which in turn will help prepare you for when real anger surfaces. In play-acting, being angry man into a mirror could make you laugh at how scary you can be, or at how ridiculous you look. Either way, it will help diffuse the anger time in remembering your angry face and not taking it so seriously. It is never too late to start play acting into the mirror. Play out the full range of your emotions, especially all your negative ones.

Lately, there has been a lot of talk about anger management. So here is foolosophy's anger management tip: <u>Making your best angry face in the mirror should become a daily ritual. Stay with it until it cracks you up. I promise that in real life it will become infinitely harder for you to maintain your anger, for you will more easily see the comedy in losing control.</u>

Chapter 6
If Ignorance is Bliss, than is Awareness Painful?

Before I became the star of my little league baseball team, my father would shout out things like, "He's no son of mine! Someone must have left him on our door step!" and, "Son, you can't play your life away or you're gonna grow up to be a bum!" Yet once I became the star of my little league baseball team, my dad would sit in the bleachers and point to the pitching mound with a proud fatherly smile telling everyone, "That's my boy, that's my son out there!"

My early awareness that I am not entirely my father's son helped me more quickly develop my sense of humor by laughing at the many differences between dad and I. Dad thought life was all about hard work. I was a prodigy of play and fun.

Realizing how different I was than my own father and mother, better prepared me for the world outside the front door. What I mean is if you are aware of the differences between you and your own family members and can find comfort in that, you will be more comfortable in the realization of how different you are from all others in the big world. With humor in mind, you can hunt for the differences; learn from the differences, be more accepting of the differences, while likewise better enjoying the differences in all people.

Yes, initially the differences may cause a certain degree of pain and discomfort, but it is humor that will enable you to transcend those differences, because it will allow you to accept them. Once you can learn to treat all differences with humor, the contrast happens. That is, ignorance becomes painful and awareness becomes bliss.

Chapter 7
The Last Romantic in Los Angeles

The day my girlfriend dumped me, I jumped in my car, drove to the beach with tears in my eyes, anger in my head, and hurt in my heart. We used to go to the beach everyday and I would push her on the swings and watch the sunset. This day I pushed an empty swing, and cried and laughed, laughed and cried, as the tears and snot drained into my mouth.

Next - insane laughter of the realization that she was gone. When the sun went down, I jumped into my car and drove to our favorite restaurant. I ordered our favorite bottle of wine, drank the entire thing myself, ordered my favorite meal as well as hers, and ate them both to really punish myself. I punish myself to learn, and I wanted to get it through my head that the relationship was really over.

Getting to your pain early, and avoiding the rush, will more quickly lead to humor development while also getting you back onto the battle field. You must be a warrior when it comes to love, for remember the old maxim comedy = tragedy + time. A foolosopher is always trying to shorten the duration of all painful experiences. Here is one more maxim of comedy for you to remember, pain + truth = funny.

Can you imagine how strange I looked to everyone in the restaurant eating both my entrée and the entrée across from me, laughing hysterically, drinking my bottle of wine all by myself? When playing the game of love do not worry about looking strange, for there has never been a normal romantic. This is what always makes it funny in the end.

Chapter 8 Speed Dating

Naturally, I could not get over my ex-girlfriend in one night, but a few months later at the super market, I met a girl that so excited me I had to approach her. I had just made a salad at the salad bar, so I grabbed two plastic forks and walked up to her and asked her if she would like to go to the beach and share my salad with me. She told me she couldn't, she didn't have time, but we exchanged phone numbers for a later date.

I called her as soon as I got home; leaving her a message about how excited I was at making her acquaintance. I called her the following day, which was a Monday, and made a date to go out that Saturday. She agreed and I hung up the phone even more excited then before.

I called her Wednesday just to talk, and she told me that she had to do a photo-shoot that Sunday. She shared her concern about going out on Saturday and that she had to get home early. I attempted to change the date so we would not be under the pressure of rushing, because a romantic does not like to be rushed, but she insisted on keeping the date.

I called her that Friday, just to confirm the time, and told her I made a reservation at my favorite Italian restaurant because food is one of my big passions as well as romance. Once more she impressed upon me the importance of getting her home early because of her big shoot the next day. This time there was even more anxiety in her voice then earlier in the week. I did not say anything to her, but I was beginning to get really irritated and starting to lose the excitement in meeting this person.

I picked her up at 7:30pm on Saturday evening, wearing my lucky shirt, and the moment I saw her, the excitement in me built up once again. I opened car door for her, and before she entered, she looked at me in the most serious fashion, and once again reminded me of how important it was that I get her home at a decent hour.

I started the car, and did not get two blocks down the street before she stressed the importance again, this time apologetically explaining to me why the date had to be so short. At this juncture I snapped mentally, and drove in silence to the Jack-In-The-Box in Santa Monica. When I pulled in the lot, she asked me what I was doing. Staring straight ahead, without saying a word, I pushed the call button, ordered four tacos, drove through, grabbed the food, and headed back towards her apartment. She kept pushing in the form of many questions regarding what I was doing. I pulled up to her house, got out of the car, still in dead silence, got the door for her once more, asked her to get out of the car, handed her the bag of tacos, and asked her if that was fast enough.

She was not happy, but I was convulsed. I got into the car without saying a word, and drove off. Now I went back to Jack-In-The-Box, got my own tacos, went to 7-11, got a six pack of beer, went home, put on the TV, ate my food and drank my beer, stewed in my anger, frustration, pain, and thought about how stupid life was becoming. To wash down my frustration, I followed my tacos with two pints of Ben & Jerry's ice cream.

No wonder America is over-weight. There are probably millions of romantics just like me who turn to food and television for solace. Maybe we can only watch romance on television, in movies, and read about it in books, because in life we are witnessing the death of romance. Romance takes time, maybe all we have time for is speed sex.

Chapter 9
The Rats are Getting Bigger, and the Maze is Getting Smaller

In my five-mile country it used to take me about forty-five seconds to get back home from my local market by car. It now takes me three hundred and twenty seconds to travel the same distance. There's ten times more traffic lights, twenty times more stop signs, endless speed bumps that never existed before, speed traps underground that won't allow you to even attain the speed limit without setting off the yellow light then the red light abruptly.

What makes this situation funny is every other car is a new or newer Porsche, Range Rover, high-end BMW, or Mercedes designed to go 180 mph. The population in what used to be a smaller town has multiplied ten times or so, and it seems someone is always pushing the crosswalk buttons, stopping the flow of traffic, or someone has already entered or about to enter one of the many new painted crosswalks.

Then there are the many idiots who step off from the curb completely blocked from view for they are sandwiched between two SUVs parked at the many new parking meters, causing me to stop abruptly because swerving is not an option for there are cars on either side of me. After my momentary anger subsides, I start laughing for I

Foolosophy

notice these people are also on cell phones, and a little too preoccupied to notice they their close proximity to a crosswalk. Obviously we must need even more crosswalks, stop signs, and signals for there are not enough of them to keep every jerk safe.

I call these people jerks and idiots because it's funny and true. They always glare at me as if I could see them, as if it was my desire to run over these checked-out, non-thinking jerks. Ironically, it's only after this unaware person causes me to have a heart attack and hit my brakes that I then entertain the thought of running them over.

My "hood" has changed in a lot of ways, and most of the changes have not been for the better. We have two local gas stations and perhaps you're old enough to remember pulling in to get your gas and having two smiling friendly people come up to your car window and ask if they could check your oil while the other pumps the gas. These days I get out of my car, walk up to thick bulletproof glass, and hand my money to a person who barely looks at me and barely speaks. I've never heard the person grunt out much more than, "How much do you want?"

After I get my gas, I then drive over to the market, where we now have security people with guns standing next to bums, street people with large cups asking for money. I tell the bums that I'd like to give them some change but I just put three dollars worth of quarters into the new parking meter (you only get three minutes for a quarter).

I get my goods out of the market, and drive home where I end up playing chicken with a couple cars on the side streets because there is now only room for one car on a two-lane road because of the hundreds of parked cars on both sides of the street. Then I have to dodge trucks larger than my house taking away dirt for the endless amount of construction taking place while other giant trucks bring wood and materials in. I do like following the roach-coaches, the many catering trucks for the smell (I love food), and I also use them as cover to lead me through these now restricted and narrow passages on the days I don't feel like playing chicken. Things could be worse I guess, I could be in the ghetto dodging bullets.

We have lost our patience with one another and this little story represents just a few examples of why. I'm sure if you take a look at your world, you can compile your own list of pet peeves that cause you mental, emotional and physical disturbance. Everyday there is a new article or two regarding what an impolite society we're becoming. Too many people and not enough space is only part of the increasing hostility, anger, rudeness, and frustration.

We're going to have to develop our individual as well as our collective sense of humor to take back our city streets. I'm writing this story because as we know humor is a funny way of talking about serious things. It has caused me pain, which of course makes me angry, to see my five mile world changing for all the wrong reasons.

Chapter 10 Pain Transference

One of the funniest, and most pathetic things that goes on in our society, is the thousands of people that walk around, drive around, attempting to transfer their pain, anger, fears, and misery onto others. I guess these people somehow feel they will have less pain if they put some, or lay some down on you and me. Or maybe it is just the old expression "misery loves company".

I love winy, unhappy, miserable people. Some of my biggest, hardest, longest laughs have come from my really depressed friends and acquaintances. This does not mean I am not a highly sensitive, compassionate, sympathetic person; it is just that a big part of comedy therapy is knowing how to tell your stories of pain and frustration without bringing the other person down, or drawing them into your nightmare.

To develop your sense of humor, you must always remember that you are telling your stories of woe to help release some pressure off of your shoulders, not transfer it to another's. The chances are extremely good that the person listening to you may have more than their fair share of pain already. We all must learn to tell our stories of pain in a humorous vain, thereby speeding up the healing process, instead of spreading the pain virus. Pain is epidemic, and may be our number one virus along with fear, stupidity, hypocrisy, and insecurity. I have done a thousand stupid things in my life, but transferring my pain to people is not on my list. As the great Oscar Wilde said[24], "Some cause happiness wherever they go, others, whenever they go." All human beings are in pain of some kind, never forget this.

Pain has always been the best teacher, and when listening to hundreds, thousands of stories of pain, you should always attempt to wear a smile on your face. I have done this most of my life, and it has confused most everyone. So I attempt to tell them, I am not laughing at you as much as I am identifying with you, relating to you, because I am human and know pain intimately. We call this empathy of a foolosopher.

Again, the great foolosopher Oscar Wilde[25], "The world has always laughed at it's own tragedies, that being the only way in which it has been able to bear them." With humor in mind, we can all be better listeners of all stories. But to really hear and feel people's pain, would simply be too painful, so you must train your magical little brain to open up, not close up, when stories of pain show up.

In today's world, pain is around every other corner in one form or another. Humor is the prepared mind, which tells us not to listen with a heavy heart, but an open mind.

---

24. Wit and Wisdom by Oscar Wilde, Dover Publications, 1998
25. Wit and Wisdom by Oscar Wilde, Dover Publications, 1998

Part V
Perception and a Healthy Mind

There is nothing funnier than people's perception of you and me; okay, there is one thing funnier than that- One's own awareness, or lack of self-awareness. This is why true humor is laughing at oneself, while real humanity is knowledge of oneself.

Humor is the key to a healthy mind for the simple reason that to know one's self is the most difficult of all things to possibly know. Humor makes self-examination and critical thinking a less fearful & painful process; this eventually moves us to a better appreciation and understanding of what it means to be a human being. Mr. Shakespeare's most accurate observation: "what fools these mortals be", has never been more appropriate than it is right now.

Chapter

1 Has Anyone Seen My Identity?

Here is a list of people's perceptions of me, identities attached to me, and some of the roles I have played on the human stage:

Fat kid, shy kid, star athlete, dumb jock, dumbest kid in school, older brother, son of great parents, son of a bitch, son of a barber, the stud, the dud, the beach bum, a nobody, a somebody, the clown, the trickster, the jester, the charmer, obnoxious guy, rude guy, an elitist, a republican, a democrat, a libertarian, mafia guy, an intellectual, a womanizer, drug addict, drug dealer, landlord, a legend, a bullshitter, liar, social butterfly, pimp, matchmaker, generous man, cheap guy, consummate actor, Confucius, confused, healer, sage, worst friend, best friend, bus boy, waiter, motorcycle salesman, car salesman, restaurant owner, laziest man on earth, mama's boy, fag, great lover, lousy lay, ripped guy, steroid guy, Socrates, Peter Pan, and my personal favorite, an alien - not from another country, not from another planet, but from another galaxy (and they were not kidding).

In Los Angeles, one can and should develop their sense of humor more quickly for this is the "land of lost identities". And thanks to Hollywood, people come from all over the world to establish their identity. Fools, freaks, fun. There is something inherently funny about people trying to find themselves, or establish an identity.

One of the major points of foolosophy is learning to laugh at identities in order to take some, if not all, the pressure off of worrying about who you are or how the world perceives you. Here is the first question I ask every fool I meet, "Do you have love in your heart?" If the person answers yes, then all you need is humor in your head to protect your heart. If the person answers no, then humor and laughter become even more important to a person who has lost that loving feeling. Love is all the confidence you need, but humor and laughter will help you fake it until love returns.

Now, you may be asking yourself what does love, or lack of love, have to do with one's identity. Answer: EVERYTHING SILLY...

If you have self-love, love period, meaning you care, deeply care, then your identity is much less complicated. If you are lacking in self-love, love for people, then your search for identity and validation could keep you in a state of dis-ease. It is why we foolosophers call humor the great healer. As important as words might be, you have to get beyond words, beyond names, even identities, if you are to have any real fun, joy, love, laughs in this life.

Chapter 2 The Adult Toy

Humor is our most important toy to keep our most important sense of play alive and well. The connection between our innate instinctual sense of play and our sense of humor is something we do not talk about and I have not seen much written about it in books, magazines, newspapers, or any publication.

What makes us human beings so special is our sense of play, and our innate ability to laugh at things that bewilder us, confuse us, and frustrate us. It is through our sense of play that we make all our human discoveries. And in order to make these discoveries less painful and scary, we have the ability to laugh and liberate ourselves from them so we can play harder tomorrow. This is how a child/fool keeps their excitement levels high. It is how I maintain and even increase my enthusiasm, passion, zest for life and all people.

A smiling mind is a mind at play. And because everything in life is a game, and everything has the play element contained within, it is humor and laughter that make game playing so much more fun and joyful. With a smiling mind, it is impossible to lose, even if you are deadly serious about everything you do. But when you take things, people, life, so seriously that you lose your sense of play, the game is over.

In present day society, we have lost our sense of play and fun, and we are all feeling the crunch. We have been "scared stupid," and fear dominates our world. Humor is the fear buster, for it is designed to make us fearless. Humor is what we have to counteract our collective fears as well as our individual fears. But what good is any toy if you do not use it, play with it, and practice with it? (In fact, take a break from this book right now, go out in public, and make a fool of yourself...)

An adult life is complicated, complex, filled with responsibilities and problems. Humor and laughter are not frivolous things. It takes emotional strength and courage to face what is in front of you. This is why I suggest facing it and looking at it through humor's vision. At any age, at any point, this is possible. We have humor and laughter available to make us more "lifeable".

If this sounds simple to you, good. Great. Wonderful. Vundabar. Stupendous. Spectacular. It is just another way we can use humor, because who does not want to make life more simple?

No one can simplify your life but you. Remember, the best part of us all is "the childlike spirit" we were all born with. So whenever you look at or interact with any other so called adult, smile broadly triggering your mind, allowing you to look at this encounter as playtime.

Now, let me show you what a giant fool I am and answer the big question:

WHY ARE WE HERE?

We are here, you fool, to play and have fun before we depart. If you don't believe me, ask any child or foolosopher.

Chapter 3
Socio-Pathetic Behavior

Perhaps you've noticed, witnessed, or read that as a society we have become more neurotic, psychotic, angry, rude, fearful, frustrated, numbed out, dumbed out, and scared stupid. Socio-pathetic is my expression for all of these ailments.

Since humor is a funny way of thinking, a funny fun way of saying, talking about serious things, it helps me to make up expressions in my head in hopes of laughing at the pain all around us which in turn helps me get out of my head. The contents of this book are here to help you do the same to better enjoy the game of life.

Like most children, I am a visionary, for we study adults, so called grown-ups, and quickly realize what is in our future. It is clear that as a society we are becoming more isolated by technology, and more mechanical like the equipment we operate all day long. People always use the expression "think outside the box". Perhaps you find this funny because the truth is most of your life is spent inside a box, staring at a box whether it be a TV, computer, cell phone, etc. And ironically we end up in a box buried under six feet of dirt. Please, do not bury yourself prematurely. Take a look at the box you put yourself in, and find the strength to break down the walls around you with humor. My hope is that this book can somehow effect, remind all adults of their original greatness.

Chapter 4
Joy Transference

You can change the chemistry in your brain everyday by simply playing against character. This means that on your worst days, days when you are in a good amount of pain, you can go out, hit the streets, and wear a bigger smile than normal.

Instead of putting on a frown, or a pained expression, wearing a large smile immediately helps you play against the negative mood you are in. This is part of the mind stretching exercise that can help you stay mentally fit, and it is the beginning of developing your sense of wit, as you move into a more positive character. As the great Oscar Wilde said, "Moods don't last. It is their chief charm." Humor and laughing at oneself merely speed up the process.

Humor is the minds way of expediting you out of a sour mood, so you can become more charming and engaging. Again, Mr. Wilde said, "It is absurd to divide people into good and bad. People are either charming or tedious." So on your worst days, it is very important to go out and practice being more playful, spontaneous, and charming. Here are some examples of what I do:

1. At my local super market, I bring back peoples shopping carts, even waiting a minute or two for them to finish unloading their groceries. Female or male, it makes no difference; I smile and say, "Pardon me, would you mind if I took your cart back for you?"

This simple little gesture shocks some people, for I live in the land of the self-absorbed, pretentious, always in a hurry, very busy, and important people. The west side of LA is also the land of entitlement. So performing any friendly move is treated with disdain and cold detachment. Still, it is worth it, for it helps me brighten my spirits, and it is even more worth it for the few who do respond favorably. Some people are even shocked that a stranger would take a moment to perform a random act of kindness, and they share their amazement with me.

2. Once again, using one of my favorite moves I stomp down my big flat foot opening the automatic sliding door for approaching people, especially the ones who find it difficult to make eye contact, and then I say, "It is a pleasure to get the door for you today!" Sometimes I would even bow, sweeping my arm and hand in an elaborate gesture saying, "Please, be my guest." Most are forced to smile, some have difficulty, but again, this does not deter me. In truth, it fuels my fire reminding me of the silly importance.

3. I roll down my window and ask the attractive girl who's on her cell phone if she could please give me her cell phone number so I can call her and take her out on the greatest date of her life. This is a fantasy joy transference.

As small and insignificant as these stories might seem, they have a much larger consequence and effect than you can imagine. For in TAKING YOURSELF OUT OF THE EQUATION, and putting your energies into doing little things for other people, you are taking your mind off of your own pain, and this is a good thing. Plus the reaction and responses will remind you of the bigger picture, and get you smiling and thinking about the world of people.

All of society represents a two-way mirror. When I walk down my neighborhood streets and look at the hostile, fearful, pained, angry expressions, this likewise makes me crack up, for I am once again reminded of the character I do not want to slip into. As bizarre as this may sound, there is nothing wrong in using a sourpuss to remind you of what you do not want to become.

<u>These silly little whimsical encounters, if practiced everyday will likewise help you get out of your own head, and make the game of life more interesting and fun.</u> Remembering that all faces are mirrors, the people that respond favorably to you help you get out of your mood, and the ones who cannot return a smile, remind you of the mood you want to leave behind. Either way, the duality of human nature can be used to better yourself through humor's vision.

In foolosophy, misery does not love company. So, in spreading joy to others instead of pain, you can more easily leave your pain behind. FOOLOSOPHY IS A DIET FOR THE MIND, and joy transference is an important part of taking your mind in the opposite direction, or out of a negative state of consciousness. In practicing doing things that get you out of your own head, you will be amazed at how quickly humor does become the personality's best friend.

Chapter 5
Truth is the Fountain of Youth

Foolosophy is the official fountain of youth. Through practicing it, you will become younger. You will return to a childlike state, and your sense of play will flourish. That is, you will become more creative, spontaneous, improvisational, curious, fearless, and hungry to learn. Childlike is how we all entered this world, and whenever you look at another so called adult, so called grownup, please remember that we all have this in common.

In practicing foolosophy and becoming younger, you must be careful not to back track, becoming childish instead. Being childish is negative destructive behavior. It is being petty, narrow minded, scared stupid, putting others down to feel important, suffering from no sense of humor, and a lost sense of play. If this is happening, then you are heading in the wrong direction. You never ever want to be childish because it will destroy your sense of play. This is precisely why we have a sense of humor. Humor protects, preserves, brightens, what is innate and great in us all, while better assisting us in dealing with falling into a childish mindset.

Childlike is being fully alive. There is no better philosophy, psychology, or self-help tool than humor. Children are born with all sorts of instinctual gifts, and humor's true beauty and purpose allows for them to be revealed.

It is that simple and that complex. The essence of humor is contrast. Children are fearless because they do not feel self-conscious about everything they do. They are uninhibited free spirits. Most adults are self-conscious and fearful. This is why children are always laughing at this unnatural behavior of adults. So in contrasting your world by fearlessly looking at the negative, humor is the bridge back to the positive.

Instead of using your pain and fears to lash out at another and be childish, take the high road and ascend by tapping into your childlike spirit. How you deal with your pain will determine how you live your life. Because humor is the great healer, when you treat your pain with it, you will always be learning and growing like a child. So negative will always become positive, adversary becomes friend, childish becomes childlike once again. The game never ends. Life is all repetition anyway. Humor keeps it new, young, and fun.

Chapter

6 A Children's Book for Adults

In the beautiful book by Peggy Jenkins Ph.D. titled, The Joyful Child[26], she has pages dedicated to the gift of laughter. She says for parents to remind their children that it is easier to smile than frown (smiling requires much fewer facial muscles). Also it is said a smile confuses an approaching frown.

Also in her book, Peggy Jenkins refers to a great sage's teachings. "Laugh your troubles away," he advises, "Laugh at mistakes and calamities. If you laugh when an earthquake begins, you can accelerate into the higher vibrations where fear cannot exist and you will simply pass it by." I too have always laughed at earthquakes, but for a different reason. The reason I love and laugh at earthquakes is I finally get a chance to meet my neighbors.

Laughter is healing. When we laugh, we are actually releasing chemicals into our bloodstream that reduce pain, and by bolstering our immune system, help prevent or cure disease. Laughter expands the lungs, clears the repertory

---

26. The Joyful Child by Peggy Jenkins Ph.D., Aslan publishing, 1996

Foolosophy

system, and provides us with extra energy. Besides contributing to our physical well being, laughter also relieves tension and diffuses many stressful situations.

Humor dissolves differences and harmonizes the atmosphere. Barriers come down and people begin to relate to one another. A favorite example of this is a true story I read in the Christopher News Notes[27] a few years back. A San Francisco policewoman was sent to investigate a family disturbance. As she approached the house, she saw a television come crashing through the window. She could hear a heated argument as she rang the bell, and a gruff voice shouted out, "Who is it?" Instead of saying "police", she responded with "TV repair man". The angry shouts dissolved into laughter and a peaceful solution was soon reached.

Henry Ward Beecher said it best when he said[28], "A person without a sense of humor is like a wagon without springs – jolted by every pebble in the road." Humor comes from our joy, and our joy is expanded by our humor. Such humor is said to be, "born of awareness of the almost universal lack of proportion in human life."

Wayne Dyer says[29] it is a parental responsibility to help children develop an ability to laugh a lot in life, to see the fun side of everything, and to be a little crazy now and then. "Make it your commitment," he urges, "to help them have as many laughs as they possibly can." Naturally, my book says the opposite. Since I was six-years-old, I've been teaching adults to laugh and play and have fun in everything we do. It's not the children who need to know these things, for them it comes natural. It is the adults who need to remember the importance of humor and laughter in their daily living.

Foolosophy is here to remind adults, parents, that it is easier to smile than frown. Being born and raised in Los Angeles, my smile has only grown broader where the hundreds of thousands of people I pass in the street seem to have lost their ability to smile at a stranger. This is part of the impetus for writing this book, for we are losing our ability to laugh, smile, and play in our neighborhood streets.

---

27. http://www.christophers.org/cnnlink.html
28. Henry Ward Beecher, Quoted in Quoteworld.org, also see: http://en.wikipedia.org/wiki/Henry_Ward_Beecher
29. KCET fund raiser

Chapter 7
The Great Healer

"Everybody becomes a healer the moment he forgets about himself" – Henry Miller

When a foolosopher recognizes a truth about who they are, what they are, how they act, behave, or misbehave, from someone mirroring their human behavior, they find it hard, if not impossible, to control an instinctual explosion that takes place inside their head. Then comes a smile. A laugh that releases the pressure locked up in their subconscious or conscious mind, because it feels so damn good. Laughter is the explosion when the truth bell has rung.

Humor is the best healer because it allows you to play doctor with yourself. And let's face it; you are the only person who can honestly, truly, heal yourself. So why not use humor and laughter to make it a lot more fun.

Laughing at oneself only requires one giant step. But once you make this initial leap, your life will be eternally changed for the better, forever. Humor is always searching for the truth, and in order to crack yourself up, you have to be willing to face as many truths about who you are as well as who you can tolerate. In the beginning this might be tough, but stick with it for self-humor is loaded with forgiveness, compassion, and yes, tolerance. From there it only gets easier and more fun as you progress and let go of these truths.

Here is a humor equation to keep in mind at all times: Without truth and the freedom to express what is locked up inside of you, there can be no real expression of love. We laugh when we hear truth, and in that momentary laughter, there is complete liberation. And also in this moment, you are in the field of unconditional love. Now can you see that sincere laughter at yourself is a shortcut to self-love?

As part of the duality of life there are going to be days when laughing at yourself is just not an option. Unfortunately, these have to exist and there is nothing that can be done about it. It's up to the individual to stay strong and push through them. NOTE: I find it helpful to beat up on myself even more, inflicting more pain into my psyche, but everyone is different. Just like we all have a self-destructive childish side, we are destined to have dark days, but oddly enough these are the days when you can best develop your appreciation and true understanding of humor.

We all have different pain thresholds, we all have different time codes, and everything depends on the severity of the pain and how long it takes to face the truth.

Chapter

8 Does My Smile Confuse You?

We have all heard the expression, "It all depends on how you look at life". Well in humors vision, life is looked at as a comedy, and I certainly hope you can surrender to this idea.

Life is drama, trauma loaded with pain, frustration, and as Horace Warpole claimed[30] in the 16th century, "To those who feel, life is a tragedy, to those who think, life is a comedy". The bad news, which is actually good news, is that we are both feeling and thinking creatures.

Pain is insane, and it is pain that will drive you insane, unless you can bravely, courageously, wisely, face your pain and learn to smile at it, laughing at the bad guy in your home movie. Yes, with humor in mind, you can be your own hero in life.

Humor helps repair your broken heart and free your soul. Many books have been written on mind, body, heart, and soul working together, so please allow me the honor and privilege of

---

30. Emotional Intelligence by Daniel Goleman, Bantam Books, 1995

adding my two cents to the pile. Thanks to humor and my ability to honestly laugh at myself and everyone I meet, I have been able to keep all four of these parts of being human alive and well.

Humor is a mind game for sure, and you do not want your intellect to get in the way of being a more loving, laughing, playful, intelligent being, tomorrow. If this sounds like a contradiction; good, for life is loaded with contradictions and when your mind is caught in one, try laughing at it to free up your head. What I really mean is there is nothing funnier in life then a know-it-all. Because when you know, truly know, there is nothing to know.

If this sounds dumb, silly, and inane to you, good. I want you laughing at me, with me, throughout this book, even if I say something really profound, prophetic, pathetic, stupid, or heavy.

In humor's vision, there is no heavy. For along with laughter, it is designed to lighten your load, not to keep a heavy heart because of a clogged overworked brain. Thinking is painful, like pretty much everything else in life, and there is no point to having humor, and your ability to think, if you are going to stay trapped in your head, which is the most painful thing of all.

Do you know why children laugh fifty to a hundred times more a day compared to adults, who maybe laugh once or twice a day? Children are not trapped in their heads yet! They have not been made to feel self-conscious, or fearful! So it is up to the adults to fully develop their individual sense of humor, as well as their collective grasp of humor, so the beautiful spirit of another generation of kids is not killed! Are you with me now?!?!?

I sure hope so, for I love children, and I have fought off every adult with humor who attempted to fill my head with crap, and kill the best part with being a human being. That is, the childlike spirit we are all born with.

Chapter 9
To Know Me is to Love You

The better you know yourself, the better you know everyone else. Remembering that we are both thinking and feeling creatures, and that to those who think, life is a comedy, and to those who feel, life is a tragedy.

Since generalizations are a part of humor, and most men (even gay men) say that women are less logical, more tenderhearted, more tactful (meaning they are taught to play nice), more social and emotional, less analytical, and definitely more inclined to take things personally, we call them drama queens. But so often men forget that all women have to be psychic, and this is why we say they are more complex creatures. For it is in their DNA, a preparation for motherhood. All great mothers are martyrs, dictators, control freaks. It is why we say women are multi-taskers, where as men are more one-dimensional, hunter-gatherers.

To make a simpler analogy, I will refer to my girlfriend's dogs. The male is named Bugsy, and the female is named Angel. Bugsy likes to sleep, eat, shit, screw, and rarely leaves his mother's/my girlfriend's side. Angel, on the other hand, is much more sensitive and aware of every sound in the house, outside of the house. She goes up to everyone more readily, sniffing them, and nervously recoiling because of her hypersensitivity, and in a doggy sense, taking everyone personally. She is also ten times better because of her power of manipulation. My girlfriend and I watch the male/female doggy roles played out and laugh all day long at the truth of their respective characters. Her dogs are a constant source of entertainment.

Likewise, for us humans, when we watch our sitcoms on television we are seeing actors play out the male/female generalizations, stereotyping them, and we laugh in our homes. The more you can find humor, consciously or unconsciously, in the truths about all human nature, the more easily you can find your own personal liberation. And the more liberation you can find in your heart, and in your head, the faster you will be able to close in on loving yourself.

Here is a generalization, stereotype, about males: We are natural fools by nature because we are the aggressors. And of a lifetime and a history of approaching females, and mostly experiencing rejection, we had to learn to adapt to this (that is, the thinking males) by laughing at ourselves to continue in our pursuit of female companionship.

Now to stay with the generalization of females, being that they are more tender hearted, more of a feeling type; they really need humor to better protect their genetic tendencies. This will free them up from taking men, other women, life, so personally.

Humor and laughter are specifically designed to allow you to look closer at both female and male genetic tendencies, as well as the bad human habits you develop along the way, helping you to escape falling prey to them. I certainly hope you can laugh, howl, at the generalizations and stereotyping I just wrote about.

Chapter 10
Humor is it

Humor is it, but unfortunately you are never going to get it, but that is okay, because the fun is in looking for it. I did not say any of this to confuse you; I said it to help you get out of your state of confusion.

All human actors, meaning all human beings, unconsciously know the importance of humor, and most know it consciously as well. The reason this is true is because without it, we would die under the weight of all our negative thoughts and feelings. Just to turning on the nightly news and seeing the horror being acted out on the world stage is pain enough for most of us, yet alone we have to deal with ourselves on a daily basis.

Pain and fear and all the other negative emotions shut us down as human beings, restricting our freedom to enjoy our day-to-day personal interactions. This reverses the life process (which is growth and evolving), and is the opposite of how we began. That is, as wide-eyed, curious, spontaneous, open minded creatures, ready and willing to receive, hungry and eager to absorb everything and everyone.

So humor is that thing that takes a person from a restricted state of consciousness to an ever-expanding state of consciousness. This automatically makes you a better human actor, for you are not afraid to be in all scenes in any life situation. Humor is the prepared mind, and a prepared mind means you can be more responsive, rather than reactive, to all life's situations. Humor helps you discover the significance in everything and everyone, especially yourself.

This is why politicians are the worst human actors. They are reactionary. What we really want from a human actor playing a politician is someone who can be responsive. Being more responsive means being quick to respond, being sensitive, being open and honest, truly listening, and having a willingness to respond. This is a real human exchange, where all actors are truly involved in the scene.

Humor is designed to make you a better actor, or if you prefer, a better human being day by day by day by day or night by night by night or day and night by day and night by day and night. Okay, I'm being a little silly, a little foolish. Because playing the role of a writer should be more playful and fun and entertaining because writing, like anything else, can be boring.

Chapter 11
It is in God's Hands

Many great healers have walked the world, but since you are the greatest healer for yourself, I am sure God would want you to develop your God-given sense of humor. God did not tell you to have that second, third piece of pie you just gobbled down, that made you sick, and added unwanted pounds to your waste line, did She?

She made laughter good and healthy and gave us nothing to laugh at but one another and ourselves to better understand the duality of our nature and the nature around us. You can thank God for the pie, but you do not want to blame God for the pie, blame mom for making the pie, blame your friend who brought you the pie, just reach down, grab your sore tummy, and share in a good belly laugh with your new wider belly. For this is just another way to seize the opportunity to develop your sense of humor.

The best way to thank God and give back is to laugh. If you want Her to hear you, laugh. If you want Her to reach out to you, laugh. The shortest distance between you and God is laughter. Children know this, adults forget this. This is probably why children do not have the desire to go to church. The easiest, shortest, most enjoyable prayer God wants to answer is laughter.

The greatest way any child can pay back their parents is by keeping humor in mind, because it is the child who ironically has to find forgiveness, compassion, and empathy for their parents as opposed to blaming them. Humor allows you to embrace the imperfections, flaws, and shortcomings of all things, because they are what teach you the greatest lessons, and allow you to grow even more. So, since we are all God's children, the greatest way to pay Her back is by keeping humor in mind.

Humor is a shortcut to truth, freedom, and love. Your mistakes allow more truth, freedom, and love to be revealed, which of course is heaven on earth. God is revealed through mistakes. Without them, you cannot truly experience God. With them, you can achieve greatness.

This is the truth, the freedom, and the love of humor. It takes us out of a painful state of consciousness, into an altered higher state of consciousness, or if you prefer, a God-like state of consciousness. Using your sense of humor keeps you in a perpetual state of prayer.

Humor is the ultimate reality check. This is the beauty of humor and our ability to laugh at ourselves daily, so we can be our own heroes. As the great poet and foolosopher James Cavanaugh said[31], "I played God today, and it was fun".

---

31. There are men too gentle to live among wolves by James Kavanaugh, Nash Publishing, 1971

Chapter

12 Programmed and Conditioned

Bob Dylan said[32], "Colleges are like old-age homes, except for the fact that more people die in colleges." An anonymous source said, "Almost everyone today is brain-damaged by our education which is designed to produce docile automatons."

From our educational systems to the world that surrounds us, we are told by mass media, and the tide of mass opinion, that we cannot survive without this watch, that car, this pair of jeans, that shirt, this make-up, to help put on our superficial mask. We're not tall enough, we're not thin enough, we're not smart enough, we're not rich enough, and we all need a title in front of our names to be important. I'm here to tell you, you only need one title so raise your hand and repeat after me:

> I AM A FOOL, I HAVE ALWAYS BEEN A FOOL, AND I CAN NOW SEE THE BEAUTY, FUN, AND PLAY THAT COMES FROM PLAYING THE FOOL. THANK YOU FOR REMINDING ME OF MY ORIGINAL GREATNESS WHICH IS THE NON-SELF-

---

32. Bob Dylan quoted in BrainyQuotes. Also see: http://en.wikipedia.org/wiki/Bob_dylan

CONSCIOUS, NON-FEARFUL, NON-INSECURE CHILD BEFORE THE WORLD HELPED ME DEVELOP ALL THESE PAINFUL PERSONALITY TRAITS. THANK YOU FOR POINTING OUT HUMOUR'S TRUE VALUE IN LEARNING HOW TO UNLEARN THROUGH LAUGHTER ANYTHING I WISH TO SHED FROM TAKING MY OWN PERSONAL INVENTORY. I WILL NO LONGER WORRY ABOUT BEING PERSONA NON-GRATA. I CAN NOW SEE THAT HUMOUR IS THE KEY FOR TAKING ALL PERSONALITY TESTS. TO THINK OF MYSELF AS SMALL AND INSIGNIFICANT IS COMEDY OF THE HIGHEST ORDER.

Chapter 13
Food For Thought

Our fast food mentality is killing us. And just like we gobble, gobble, gobble our food to more quickly get back to work, watching television (which involves more gobbling), we likewise gobble up one another and joke about everything from our short and growing-shorter attention spans, to the truth that we have less and less time for one another and the things that really feed us.

When you start devouring people like you do food, you will suffer indigestion of the heart and head. I write these stories because humor tries to say serious things in a funny way. The problem is it is not very funny how we treat one another in this sped up world. There are little nutrients in fast food, just like there is little meaning and content in brief human encounters lacking in any substance and/or sustenance.

Everything is food, and people take time to digest if we are to extract the richness out of them.

Chapter 14
What Makes a Personality Great?

A healthy, playful, intelligent, sense of humor is my answer to this most important question. This is what makes a great foolosopher as well. It is adopting and using the positive aspects of humor, not the negative. Humor, like everything else, has a duality to its nature. The best part of using humor is your personality type does not matter. A sense of humor really means that you have a better sense of oneself, a better appreciation and understanding of who you are and what you are about. It makes self-awareness, self-knowledge, and self-appreciation more fun.

Foolosophy is designed to fully resurrect, revive, reawaken, and refresh the life in you. If we are here to fully live, and foolosophers know we are, humor makes looking like a fool at everything we do, less embarrassing and less painful so we can keep moving forward while shedding more and more of our hang ups and fears.

Every child born on earth has a sense of humor, for we come into this world unselfconscious, and then the world outside begins to make us feel more and more self-conscious about pretty much everything. At its best, humor is our mind asking us to find the courage to laugh at as much of our self-conscious behavior as possible in order to be free.

Chapter 15
For Women

Ladies, please look at the female characteristics you were genetically given (your genetic tendencies), and use humor to self liberate, self medicate, knowing laughter is the best medicine on the way to loving yourself for all the right reasons. I'm going to make some female generalizations so please remain calm remembering that generalizations are a part of humor.

Females are multi-taskers. They have to be able to do eight things at once. Women are also psychic for they are the primary parent and need to know what is to come. Psychic women are misinterpreted by non-thinking males as not very nice. This is the contrast of humor, psychic/psycho. We humans have humor to view our differences, embrace our differences, accept our differences, and laugh at our differences.

Humor is the buffer between men and women. If women can truly get in touch with their sense of humor, then the real woman's liberation can take place. No movement will truly liberate women unless humor is in the equation. I was told one of the leaders of the feminist movement said, "We're becoming the men we hate." I find it funny how all movements go to extremes. Again, humor is the balance for us when we need to look at extreme behavior.

We males are fools from early on doing anything, everything, to impress you females. You laugh at us when you gather together, and keep on laughing at us for the fools we are, but now it's time for you to spend more time reflecting on your own psychic, psycho behavior to better know your own duality. Accept foolosophy and develop the same sense that you most admire in a man. Through humor's vision we can have true equality because you will see the fun lies in our inequalities.

Women are becoming men; men are becoming women, what the hell is going on? I want to keep my manlihood. Please keep your feminine qualities, keep your loving, caring, nurturing ways. Just develop your sense of humor and you shall have your independence. No man or woman is truly free without it. No sex change, no make over, no human is complete without humor's inner-transformation and understanding.

> "You'd be surprised how much it costs to look this cheap." – Dolly Parton

Part VI
Life is All Improvisation

Life is all improvisation. We are all selling something, and always developing our personalities; humor is the personality's best friend. Be sure to make a mental note that humor is the tool that keeps all communication and all human interaction alive and well. Our humor keeps the flow between us rolling along lively and playful so that listening becomes as much fun as talking.

This book is only as good as the reader. I make this statement early on in order to test my reader's sense of humor; however, you get the last laugh on me, even if you were foolish enough to buy this book.

Chapter 1
Attention

Every human being comes into this world seeking attention. We live in a world of people starving for attention. With humor in mind, you can give all people the proper attention, while still paying attention. Really listening to people, really paying attention will be painful at first, but eventually, inevitably, you'll learn.

When people ask me how they can more quickly develop their sense of humor, I smile and tell them this: Sit with as many people as you can face-to-face, and really struggle in your attempt to digest, ingest, what is being communicated. The most important skill for all actors on stage, television, or film, is their ability to listen. This applies to us human actors on the world stage.

I come from a long lineage of bad listeners, and naturally, I too became inflicted with the disease. But what I discovered in a lifetime of listening to most adults is that you should not listen to most adults. This is because very few adults have a sense of humor about themselves (which in turn, only makes them more laughable). Children call these types of adults' stiff, boring, rigid, unplayful, uninteresting, joyless dweebs. Please do not take this personally, or be offended if you feel you fall into one, two, or all of these categories.

I call this to your attention because children are our most important asset; however, people remain important as well even if they are checked out adults. Humor is all about stopping unhealthy trends, sub-planting them with a healthier, wiser way of living.

Here is another tip for paying attention with humor in mind: When you look at all so called grownups, smile, remembering that somewhere locked up in their bigger bodies is a seven year old boy or girl dying to come out and play with you and have some fun.

This is not a joke, I do this constantly, for I am always looking for playmates in my neighborhood streets, but it is getting harder and harder to find big kids to play with. Do I have to wait until 5 pm to go to happy hour at my local tavern bar or restaurant, and get high before I can have some fun? Humor is, and should be, our natural drug of choice. If you chose to use it, then acting drunk all day is a blast. Only you do not have to slur your words, or stagger down the street. Acting drunk is a state of mind that belongs to humor. So you will not have to drink and do all sorts of drugs to deal with the pain that comes with adulthood. Please, give yourself the proper attention by using your own sense of humor daily. Attention is time, and time spent laughing at yourself will lead to true liberation.

Chapter 2 Intention

My intention for laughing at my mom, dad, everyone I am close to, is because I wanted to remain close to them. Sound weird to you? It is the beautiful irony of humor and laughter that I am teaching you in this book.

The people, the things you love most in your life, and want to continue to love most in your life, require even more humor development. For it is the things you love, the people you love, that will drive you most crazy, insane, if you cannot laugh at them.

Nobody teaches you this in any school or college, yet deep down, instinctually everybody knows it. It is the love/hate joke that none of us understand. It is the simple/complex duality of life. What we do understand is that nothing is more draining than hate, anger, and pain. So this means that nothing is really funny until we show the maturity that comes from humor's wisdom in pushing through the pain that is somehow attached to love.

The great foolosopher Oscar Wilde said, "Love is a mutual misunderstanding". What little understanding I have about love is this: I need humor and laughter to make it less painful. Pain, hate, and anger are draining, laughter and humor is highly sustaining (hey, I think I made a little rhyme).

Humor is the brain's filter to help you keep your head clear, and your heart open. Use your sense of humor when trying to discover another's intention. If it is to feel superior to you, I say go belly up, surrender. Support the small-minded childish imp. For chances are you are not going to open their mind, but more importantly, you do not buy into their narrow mindedness. Instead, use this opportunity to increase you sense of humor by realizing what a chump you have standing before you.

Life is a poker game. Learn to read people while having more fun playing the game, but never go "all in" without the ability to laugh at yourself after you lose a hand or two, or a hundred. In all games, and especially in the big game of life, humor is the high road, and no one escapes the low road.

Chapter 3
I'm Just Kidding

A hundred, a thousand, two thousand times in your life, you will hear someone say to you or someone else after they make the comment that they were only kidding. <u>Just remember, they are not kidding, for there is truth in the expression "I'm kidding".</u>

Human beings are always struggling to use humor in many different and varied forms to soften or mask something that might be bothering them. This is okay, and you should not take it personal. This is something we humans do because we feel uncomfortable with harsh truths, and for that matter, any truth at all.

"I'm kidding" is a follow up to some form of us attempting to deliver truth. "I'm kidding" turns any sentence into a joke, and all jokes have some truth to them because humor is always searching for truth. Some jokes can be highly offensive, insensitive, and may hurt. When one of these jokes crosses your path, please remember that the person's intention is usually not to hurt you, but rather an attempt to make you laugh.

When you hear someone say to you, "I'm kidding," smile and thank them for whatever information they are struggling to convey, knowing that there is a component of truth in it and that they are trying to be human and kind. This is just another form of human play, and with your ever-developing sense of humor, you will not be offended.

Likewise, this will keep a smile on your face, maybe even make you chuckle, when you follow up using the words, "I'm kidding" to more gingerly convey your own thoughts and feelings. This is humor's way of keeping human improvisation open. Because in life, most of us are better at repressing, suppressing things, whereas humor is always trying to open us up to keep the action, dialog, flowing free. Humor is the adult toy/tool to perform at one's optimum in life.

Chapter 4
Love is All the Confidence You Need

If there is anything that deserves to be called miraculous, is it not love? What other power, what other mysterious force is there which can invest life with such undeniable splendor? The miracle which everyone is permitted to experience sometime in his life, the miracle which demands no intervention, no intercession, no supreme exertion of will, the miracle which is open to the fool and the cowards as well as the hero and saint, is love – born of an instant, it lives eternally.
Henry Miller [33]

If love makes the world go around, then it is humor's task to make sure we stay on our axis. It's all down hill after little league, or, it's all uphill after little league...

No matter how you deliver a line of thought, if there is love contained within, and humor in mind when delivering a thought as well as receiving one, you are perpetually covered, or in a state of foolosophy.

---

33. Nothing But The Marvelous by Henry Miller, Capra Press, 1991

Everything I love has brought me a ton of pain, suffering, frustration, with a dash of anger. It is humor that allows us human beings the best shot at dealing with our thoughts and emotions to keep love supple and strong.

Courageous strength of character and a whole lot more goes into a constantly evolving sense of humor. Learning and growth as a character, a personality, with more and more developing of character, never rest in a foolosopher's soul. As I write this, I am so fatigued mentally, emotionally, I can barely put pen to paper. I am just doing what we foolosophers do best. I am pushing through my discomfort and pain on my way to smiling and laughing at whatever the outcome of this book is. If it ends up in the trash like 98.3% of all the other stuff I have written, so be it.

You could say that 98.3% of my life has been a waste. Most likely, this would be an accurate appraisal of my accomplishments in society's eyes. But thanks to humor's range and my life long love affair with laughing at myself, I feel like the most successful child ever placed on Earth. <u>This is because evolving foolosophers understand that you grow younger, wiser, and more loving with every mistake you make.</u>

The expression "You can learn from your mistakes" translates in foolosophy to "You can learn a lot faster by quickly laughing at your mistakes." This in turn prepares your mind for future failings. A foolosopher knows hindsight is not 20/20 like we have been told. We humans have a tendency to compound our stupidity. Our history is replete with supposedly the best and brightest among us making giant mistakes over and over and over again.

If you do not believe me, just take a look at politics. Comics that make fun of, point out political stupidity, insanity, know how easy this is (it's like stealing). However, they do this to help us find strength and courage in our collective laughter. Politicians rarely, if ever, leave their bias or money base. And let me generalize about American politicians. They are a bunch of humorless jerks that we must all rise above to live. History repeats itself; life is loaded with repetition, and humor makes repetition more improvisational and fun. If you love politics, or politicians (which is just another game), you need a sense of humor to watch all businesses functioning. Otherwise you will blow your brains out.

Chapter 5
I Love Humor

If love is the most important thing, then humor is the second most important thing, for there is no real self-love, or love for anyone else without the presence of humor. Please keep this in mind, for humor is the ultimate mind game we instinctually discover and use to keep love alive and well. <u>You will never think of humor in the same way after reading and absorbing this book.</u>

Why? You ask. Because humor is not about telling funny jokes, or even being funny. There is nothing funny about life until you filter it, process it in humor's vision. We are all old enough now (assuming you are over the age of 16) to know that life is frustrating, aggravating, scary, and painful. My motto is "get your pain early and avoid the rush". A lot of people drink, do drugs, pop pills, live in denial, stay really busy, in hopes of never facing pain or reality. Me? I like my pain straight, right between the eyes. Pain makes you cross-eyed; you have blurred vision from tearing up. Your head feels like it is about to implode from rationally attempting to decipher why God gave us pain.

Pain is the price we pay for pursuing pleasurable things, such as love. As a romantic, I've had my heart broken, busted into 1000 pieces, a hundred different times or more. But like the song lyrics go, "Fools rush in where wise men never go, but wise men never fall in love so how are they to know?" For me, pain is the great teacher, and humor is the great healer.

Humor is more important than most people consciously understand. Unconsciously however, I feel most people do understand its true purpose and value. <u>Life itself becomes more pleasurable when keeping humor in mind.</u> Because of it, I can truly say I love life, I love people, I love writing. And nothing in my life has been more painful to me than writing, for I had to go deeper and deeper into my head, heart, and soul to seek out the passion, respect, and love humor has to offer.

Only a giant fool would attempt to write a book describing the pleasure, freedom, joy, fun, and self-love that comes from being able to laugh at oneself. It is the shortcut to love, so learn to laugh at yourself in pursuing everything you hope to love.

Today, our modern world is "Screw You with love." Everyone lives by different rules. Humor only has one rule: Keep opening your mind to better deal with, even enjoy, the narrow minded, small minded, close minded, mindless people that inhabit the same planet we all share. A trip to the market can be an eye opening experience provided you open them. In my eyes, I always witness the modern day Shakespearean characters I call Oblivious and Oblivia. These are the men and women who gather their goods reaching over you, around you, or physically bump into you, without a trace of awareness or a personality to match.

I run into them again in the checkout line, only this time they are usually standing on my left foot anxiously attempting to hurry me along so they can shove their credit in and get out. In this case I smile at Oblivia and say, "Excuse me, I'm so sorry I wear a size 16 shoe and my big flat feet are always getting in people's way. Please allow me to remove it from under your foot. I wouldn't want to cause you anymore discomfort than I already have by my presence in line."

These are my responses to living in the modern world. I'm dead serious, and the people who know me know what I am capable of. We need more fearless social warriors willing to wake the rude, checked out, impatient characters like Oblivia and Oblivious. Remember to always maintain your smile, be cool, and be responsive rather than reactionary. I know, easier said than done, but with a little practice it really does stray from an act of futility.

The truth is, I'm writing this book because I'm losing my own patience, experiencing more frustration and anger then ever before (this may be the first "help-me" book to exist). But it has taught me and continues to teach me everyday to be unafraid of looking at the negative in all things, in all people, in myself.

No matter how you interpret this book, my stories, thoughts, opinions, catchphrases, it is all about turning the negative into a positive as quickly as possible. Sometimes you have to force a smile even when you're in a negative place to help trigger your mind out of that tight spot. I'm asking a lot when I ask for your help, but now more then ever we need it. Please, learn to love humor as I have and accept all that it will reveal.

Chapter 6
May I Be Partially Honest With You?

In your daily conversations please use expressions like this to help you keep, as well as develop further, your own sense of humor. This will help you qualify where the person you're attempting to engage, to connect with is at. Humor allows all personalities breathing room. You and I have to cut through the political correctness in our social emotional and mental intercourse, and it's keeping humor in mind that allows for this human ebb and flow.

Political correctness is the major cancer that is contributing to the human shutdown. The reason my life has been so rich is because I could engage, really listen to all kinds of people and not be offended by anything they said. As I reflect back on my life, I realize this helped me learn more and more each day about what it means to be human. This meant that all human exchanges for me were a lot more fun for I could enjoy all the different thoughts and ideas that remain inside the heads and hearts of most individuals. This is the expanding consciousness of humor that is described throughout this book.

Since the universe is at play all around us, we should want to keep our mind in the same state. Just imagine the fun to be had by allowing people to let their real thoughts and emotions come out. Humor is humanities coming out to party. Why should all the gays and lesbians have all the fun coming out, what about all the normal people?

By the way, I've never met a normal person. But I have met a lot of boring people, people with a restricted consciousness; individuals who revel in being myopic, narrow-minded and close-minded. These are the people who brought us political correctness. In humor's vision, there is no such thing as normal. By this I mean, humor allows for all acceptance. It is the compassion we are all really looking for, the empathy we are all really looking for, realizing more of our similarities, as scary as this may sound.

Yes, real maturity is keeping your wits and your sense of humor handy when engaging all types of people. This means you are sensitive, but you are also sensible. It is truly allowing the individual in front of you to be true and emote honestly. Please remember that emotions rule our lives, so if we are not allowed to honestly and truthfully express all that is inside of us, then how are we to fully live, play, and have fun in this life?

Without truth, and the freedom to express it, there can be no real love. So who's kidding who? What we really want to say to the people we care about is, "I'm not afraid of you," which is even more potent than, "I love you". For "I'm not afraid of you," means, "I have a sense of humor and you may truly speak what is on your mind."

Sometimes there will be an initial sting from the pain and anger that comes from hearing the truth, but you can always end up laughing at it, and it will becomes easier and less painful the more you practice hearing it. Humor says if something tastes bad spit it out. It's like the old fart joke, there's more room on the outside. This may be bathroom humor, but in a piece this serious you have to have a little fun.

The reason "may I be partially honest with you" makes you smile is because we go through our days and nights suppressing most of what's inside of us for fear of offending someone, or exposing our deep dark feelings. This is why laughing at oneself is so cathartic. It feels so good when you can laugh at the truth about who you are. This means that even if you can't find people to be truly honest with, you can at least sit alone with yourself and use humor to make your soul searching a healthier endeavour, not such a heavy painful thing. Does this make sense to you?

Because humor is always struggling to help us make sense out of everything that is painful to us. Because humor is about having a better sense of oneself, a better sense of who it is you are. In the beginning, you may not find this to be funny because there is nothing funny about suppression, repression, and depression, is there?

You know what is funny about this piece? I'm being more than partially honest with you. Please keep in mind that humor is always struggling to help us breakdown the complexities of life, the complexity that is our world, the complexity that is our mind, to make things simple once again.

Chapter 7

Have an Awful Day

Instead of saying, "Have a nice day," try saying, "Have an awful day," just to see if the person is paying attention. You would be amazed at how many people respond with "Thank you" and move on. I'm serious! We are so preoccupied, so checked out, so busy or bored, or in such a hurry, that we need to help one another in the field of play. Our playground is being condensed and we are seeing a personality shutdown!

"I distrust the perpetually busy; always have. The frenetic ones, spinning in tight little circles like poisoned rat. The slower ones, grinding away their foursore and ten in righteousness and pain. They are the soul-eaters." – Mark Slouka[34]

This book is about "comedy therapy" in the streets. When you think fun, it pushes you to be the creative child you once were and can be again. To live in a cliché is boring; it kills the best part of us all. It is time to become fearless like the child, engaging each other in a playful way, bringing back fun into our social politics in the streets.

---

34. Blog post by Mark Slouka: http://tinyurl.com/2yocgv

At your local market, bank, gas station, you are bombarded with "Have a nice day." You are not a damn parrot, or a robot (yet). Try saying, "Have a beautiful thirty-seven-and-a-half-hours," or "It has been a pleasure having you pass through my line of vision," or "Thank you for allowing me to see you for the first time."

<u>Children say the silliest, wisest, stupidest, cleverest, dumbest, most wonderful things.</u> We must learn from them, and unlearn what we have learned from the social retardation of adults. You can use the titles and definitions found in this book to help unlearn these bad habits. Use them, but also be creative and inventive yourself (I don't want my titles becoming cliché). Follow your mood in the moment. It is the idea of play and fun for adults that we are after.

For example, a big brute of a guy with an unpleasant expression on his face is about to enter the supermarket before me. I quicken my pace from the opposite end, grabbing his attention, and beat him to the automatic door. When I arrive I stomp down my size 16 shoe to open the door, put a big smile on my face, and say, "Allow me to get the door for you, don't you love automation?" The big guy's expression changes as he is literally forced to smile from the sheer silliness of the moment and actually thanks me.

This move also works great on women. Try it and say, "Chivalry is not dead! After you, Madame!" Older ladies love this and seem to be the most playful, most responsive, and most fun. People want to connect.

Most of the thoughts in this book are different, or in opposition to most of what you have been taught. Remember, you must use fun and your sense of play to counter what you have been told, or that has been drilled into you by the masses. Use fun to fight fear. If you understand this simple message, you are not dead yet and there is still hope. This is good news.

Chapter

8 Call Me a Fool

The definition of a fool according to Ambrose Bierce from his book The Devil's Dictionary[35] is:

Fool, n. A person who pervades the domain of intellectual speculation and diffuses himself through the channels of moral activity. He is omnific, omniform, omnipercipient, omniscient, omnipotent. He it was who invented letters, printing, the railroad, the steamboat, the telegraph, the platitude, and the circle of the sciences. He created patriotism and taught the nations war – founded theology, philosophy, law, medicine, and Chicago. He established monarchical and republican government. He is from everlasting to everlasting – such as creations dawn beheld he fooleth now. In the morning of time he sang upon primitive hills, and in the noon day of existence headed the procession of being. His grandmotherly hand has warmly tucked-in the set sun of civilization, and in the twilight he prepares man's evening meal of milk-and-morality and turns down the covers of the universal grave. And after the rest of us shall have retired for the night of eternal oblivion, he will sit up to write a history of human civilization.

---

35. The Devil's Dictionary, Ambrose Bierce, NuVision Publications, 2007

Since the fool is the most important role you or I could ever play on the human stage, and because I had to look up these words not knowing what they meant, here is Merriam-Webster's definitions of the bigger words in the above description to further explain our greatest role:

Omniscient: (1) having infinite awareness, understanding and insight (2) possessed of universal or complete knowledge

Omnipotent: (1) almighty (2) having virtually unlimited authority or influence

Because I could not find omnific, omniform, and omnipercipient, a fool's guess at these definitions would be that they could only mean more greatness and freedom by making a fool of yourself.

For contrast sake, here is Merriam-Webster's definition of the fool you do not want to be, but unfortunately will play out on rare occasions:

Fool: (1) a person lacking in judgment and prudence (2) a harmlessly deranged person or one lacking in common powers of understanding

The reason we love playing the fool is because it leads to folly. Here is the definition of folly according to The Devil's Dictionary:

Folly, n. That "gift and faculty divine" whose creative and controlling energy inspires man's mind, guides his actions and adorns his life.

This will keep alive your sense of play, spontaneity, and ability to improvise in all life situations as you grow.

Chapter 9

"Fools Anonymous" - 12 Step Program

Thoughts become actions, and actions become habits. Here is a lesson in simple psychology: Negative thoughts lead to negative habits; positive thoughts lead to positive habits. With this in mind, begin practicing our motto – TAKE EVERYTHING AS A COMPLIMENT. Positive habits will soon develop, for this simple thought has life-altering potential.

Example: Someone says to you, "You have a big nose!"

Reach up, grab your nose, move your fingers all around the perimeter, massage it for a second, put a huge smile on your face (validating the infantile comment), and say, "Thank you, thank you very much." In humor, you own every moment by turning all negative moments inside out, upside down, all around. As fools, we can rarely change the opinions or perceptions of others. The best we can do is confuse them, keep them guessing, catch them off guard, keep them off balance…

Example #2: Someone says, "Boy are you fat!"

Put your left hand on your belly, raise your right hand and point to your head, and say, "Thank you! I'm not only fat, but I'm stupid too!" It's back to the basics we were never taught as kids. The ability to utilize humor is proportional to the amount of attention paid to the stupidity of yourself and others, and to the amount of fun had in reflecting, storytelling, and acting upon such observations.

To assist us all in our attempt to develop the habit of humor, there are twelve steps to "Fools Anonymous" (based off of <u>Twelve Steps and Twelve Traditions</u>[36]):

1. 1.We admit we are powerless over what spills out of the mouths of our fellow man, and that we, as people, are all basically unmanageable.
2. We have come to believe that humor is more powerful than anyone's ability to put us down, and can always be used to restore our sanity.
3. We have made a decision to turn our attention and abilities in the direction of play and fun as we remember it to have been when we were children.
4. We have made a searching and fearless moral inventory of our loss of play and fun as we have grown into adulthood.
5. We have admitted to God, to ourselves, and to anyone who had, or took the time to listen, the exact nature of our contribution to the decline of fun and play in our society, and have embraced the task of reversing this trend.
6. We are entirely ready to laugh at all defects of character, our own and others.
7. We humbly remember that no one can put us down but ourselves.
8. We are always ready to make amends for the sole purpose of the preservation of fun.
9. We always take the direct approach to fun, if and only if, the play is not intended to hurt any involved party.

---

36. Alcoholics Anonymous, AA World Services Inc., 1976

10. We take everything as a compliment. We quickly forgive, and quickly apologize to everyone, including ourselves.
11. We have realized through observation the power of fun, play, and laughter, while appreciating the maturity involved and compassion required in playing the fool.
12. Having a reawakening of fun in our lives, we have realized the positive results of dealing with the negative in a positive way. We have learned it is difficult to hate yourself or others when you are having fun.

Chapter 10
Exercising One's Personality

Yoga For the Mind

Humor opens us up and makes us more flexible in our head, making us more creative, improvisational in all of life's moments. This is the ultimate objective of foolosophy. We're trying to make the small little encounters throughout the day a little more enlivened for the fun of it. Here are some examples of the mundane boring questions asked of us daily and some answers I've given to them (feel free to use them but it is much more fun to be spontaneous and make up your own depending on how you feel at that moment):

How are you? How ya doin?

1. I'm still erect (This is especially effective and silly when you are responding to a female)
2. They'll never take me alive!
3. If I were any worse, I'd be dead...

What do you do (for a living)?

1. I'm a lion tamer, but lately I've been thinking about herding sheep
2. I sell used underwear, it's a dirty business but somebody has to do it
3. I drink (then head abruptly for the bar if applicable)
4. Absolutely nothing, and I'm very good at it (this response is not cherished by most of the women in LA)

What's your sign (astrological)?

1. Keep off the grass
2. For Sale (meaning your available for dating, romance, love, sex)
3. Sold (as in your spoken for)
4. Temporarily Out of Order / Closed For Repairs

You are looking for the humor in every situation for this is how you better develop your sense of humor. The rearrangement of words and thoughts that stray from the typical will help you be creative, more alive, and less mechanical. Likewise it not only works for you, but will also work to alert the other person that you are open to an improvisational exchange.

If funny things pop out of your mouth and your head, then you have a better chance at having the person across from you return the playful fire. People will see from you giving a more fun silly response that you do indeed have a sense of humor, and likewise will be able to tell from their response if they are receptive and have a sense of humor as well.

You may feel uncomfortable at first, silly with these responses, and yes, some people will look at you strangely, but fear not, just tell them you are working on your sense of humor. If you feel like a fool, Good! That's the whole point silly! Accept it.

We need to learn to have more fun in our social, emotional play. We should be looking for fresh ways of interacting on our way to eventually telling the truth about what it is we do, what sign we are, and how we are doing. To play is to be free from all the restrictive, typical, boring repetitions life has to offer.

Play and humor make us flexible, not rigid and robotic, in our responses. Rearrange your words and thoughts in a more playful way and alert the world you are not dead. If you need to (as I've done hundreds of times), tell the person you are just playing with them, having some fun. You will soon realize the importance of humor and play in everything we do.

Just like children do, play is experimental. This is the fun of humor for it allows us to be more improvisational in all aspects of life, in all social forms. "Play is without Why" says Stephen Nachmanovitch[37]. It's our original spontaneous character. It's the fool we all were before becoming self-consciousness, and having to worry about how we are being perceived.

A playful mind is a liberated mind. A liberated mind is a mind that understands the importance of humor. And no one understands the importance of humor and play better than a fool. So the next time someone asks you what you do, what sign you are, or how you're doing, maybe your answer should be that you're a fool for play just trying to have some fun.

---

37. Free Play by Stephen Nachmanovitch, Penguin Putnam Inc., 1990

Chapter 11
Jump For Joy

A foolosopher is someone who regards the entire world as their home. A foolosopher is someone who uses humor to get out of their head and into the beautiful game called life. A foolosopher is someone who uses humor and laughter to be more comfortable in their own skin. A foolosopher is someone who fearlessly looks into the mirror each and everyday and finds the strength to laugh at the image staring back at them. A foolosopher is someone that takes all criticism as a compliment. A foolosopher is someone that uses humor to better able themselves to know what to look at, what to pay attention to, as well as what to let go of. A foolosopher is someone who never uses the expression self-esteem. A foolosopher is someone who knows the importance of staying animated, curious, and excited upon meeting anyone and everyone and never being intimidated or frightened by them. A foolosopher is someone who knows that in the world of cause and effect if someone is causing them pain and discomfort to use humor and go belly up and the effect will not be so great. A foolosopher is someone who knows their sense of humor protects their sense of play, and their sense of play is the road to joy. A foolosopher is someone who experiences perpetual goose bumps, for every moment in life is stimulating. A foolosopher is someone who knows that much of life is unlearning, undoing, to return to our original greatness.

The time to acknowledge joy has come. Fear is a great place to hide, but in life's game of hide-and-seek, it is only fun if you are found. Remember back as a child laughing when you were found, discovered? To discover joy is to return to a state of oneness with the Universe. Joy has been called the greatest attainment in life. It is our birthright, and comes from that intangible area called our soul.

"There is a misconception that happiness and joy are one and the same. Happiness has its seat in the emotions. It is a reaction of the personality and occurs when the personality experiences conditions that satisfy its emotional nature. Joy is a quality of the soul, and according to the sages, it is realized in the mind when the personality and the soul are in harmony. Joy is untouched by circumstances, whereas happiness is affected by what goes on around us. Joy grows in spite of conditions. Happiness does not. One can be in joy while unhappy. For instance, one can have pain and distress but feel the pure joy of "being," the awareness of Universal Love." – Peggy Jenkins, The Joyful Child[38]

Remember: Happiness is not a destination; it's a way of traveling. Whenever you travel take your sense of humor, which is nothing more than the right mental attitude. This should lead to an experience of much more happiness.

One should strive to become a fool on the level of the personality, a foolosopher on the level of the soul, and find harmony between them through humor. It is then, that a joyful state can be reached.

A little poem from the biggest foolosopher,

Intense pleasure
Intense pain
Oh
The
Joy

---

38. The Joyful Child by Peggy Jenkins, Aslan Publishing, 1996

Chapter

1 Conclusion: The Last Laugh...

"Some laugh at others, and some are laughed at by others; those who laugh at others also become the butt of other's laughter while those who are laughed at in turn laugh at others. Ah, people will never stop laughing at one another, will they? There's still all the rest of that one great treasury of the laughable – the whole world past and present with you and me in the middle of it as well, as part of the pabulum. Man isn't man without talk, and talk's unthinkable without laughter. Yes, the world wouldn't be the world without talking and laughing. Ah, cloth-bag monk, Maitreya the Laughing Budda, my master! Yes, you are my master!" – Feng Menglong (1574-1646)

...A foolosopher always has the last laugh on themselves, which is always the best laugh of all!

Appendix A
Official Foolosophy Dictionary

These definitions represent various life situations and the way to cope with each. Such situations are random, and we do not know what to expect regardless of how well prepared we might be for any given situation or predicament. Humor is the closest thing we have to indiscriminate and all-encompassing life preparation.

This dictionary has no direction. It is comprised of random stories, riddles, ideas, titles, opinions, perceptions, contradictions, interpretations of my own and many others' thoughts and feelings, all to help me explain why humor is our greatest gift in keeping individuality while still enjoying group mentality.

A Baby's Stare: Be forever the observer

America Needs a Good Spanking: Humor to kick and kiss butt, for we are all adults now???

Are You Laughing at Me?: This is not a question, rhetorical or otherwise. NEVER USE THIS SENTANCE! You will never again be bothered or worried by this contemplation once you have absorbed the role humor must play in our lives. You want people to laugh at you, silly!

Back to Greatness: Part of humor's range is to explore the dark side of human nature to help free us from ourselves. With humor you may travel anywhere, everywhere, and you don't have to be afraid of being seen with anyone. You learn to trust your own judgment while developing your own character. Humor taps into our nature while distilling, deflecting, and digesting people's character, or lack of character.

Be Your Own Hero: Humor makes leaders of us all, for we don't need more sheep in this world. Forget the Flock.

Beepers, Creepers: As part of a modern technological society in which we are continuously attempting to increase and improve our standard of living, our gadgets ironically appear to be diminishing our quality of life. We must begin to eliminate these non-essentials to increase the potentials for fun and self-fulfillment. Our technological accomplishments are not impressive, but depressive.

Beyond Genius: A true foolosopher is not trapped by his talents, abilities, or genius. She has the ability to laugh at her gifts as easily as her defects.

Beyond Words: Use humor to protect you from the error that often occurs from mind to mouth.

Business Cards: If you hand out your card to a member of the opposite sex expecting a phone call and a subsequent date, forget it, take it back, and use only for business. A lesson learned the hard way by many hopeful young members of the work force supplied for the first time with this new form of ID.

Checked Out: Zombie, Comatose... The following words and definitions apply to someone "Shut Down" or "Checked Out":

1. Inured – to accustom, especially to something unpleasant
2. Apathy – lack of interest or concern, which leads to...
3. Ignore or Ignoring

When you see someone either shut down or checked out, recommend this book to bring them out of this state.

Closed on Account of Repairs: On bad days, use this title (or something like it) as both a reminder to others of your condition and a negative mood buster to get your mind on humor. You must be your own best friend in these down moments, allowing for self-repair while also giving others a playful cue as to what you need from them at such times.

Comedy Therapy: The goal of this book is to provide this service. That is, to open your mind, repair your broken heart, free your soul.

Dancing, Singing: Nobody is ever angry or upset when they are singing or dancing. Next time you're upset, go to your room and sing or dance no matter what. Chances are you'll end up embarrassing yourself, which is great!

Distraction Disorder: A bad case of the double D. Maybe the word angst came from these additions that forever interrupt and complicate our lives. What used to be our 10 minute attention span has now became an 11 second attention span... and we want meaning in our lives?!

Does My Smile Confuse You?: This title may be applied to numerous situations, as everyone seems to have a hidden agenda. But when there is no hidden agenda and your smile is sincere, people appear to not understand. Do not despair, if your smile is sincere and it is the very same smile you have had all your life, let no one take it from you. Wear it proudly, as it is a unique expression of who you are.

Don't Worry, You'll Feel Better When You Get Well: Have lots of fun with this one – use often. It is highly effective if you are fed up with whiners. It's particularly effective with even the most vigilant hypochondriacs! Take the humor pill and call me in the morning. It is the best antidote to the various ills of the human predicament. Just ask your subconscious.

Einstein Versus Frankenstein: Humor works best in viewing the duality of our nature.

Equality: Only in humor's vision do we have true equality. We are all cartoons.

Everyone is Selling Something: The difference between seduction and sexual harassment is salesmanship. We're selling humor in all transactions.

Everyone was Wrong: Learn to dismiss criticism, and learn what it's like to be the only one who is right!

Foolosophy: The solution to evolution. Laughter is the child of surprise. See book.

Going Nowhere Fast: With humor in mind, you can make yourself the most successful person ever, even if you never get out of your lazy boy chair. If you don't mind reading a book written by a nobody (or a "bum" as my father referred to me), then you should find this book interesting. I make fun of the very thing I am writing about because it is so important to have the capacity to let go (even of the things you love the most).

Grow Up: We have a society of childish, petty, infantile, mental midgets, who need to grow up remembering that real maturity lies in the ability to laugh at oneself after acting like a rude imbecile. Males dominate in this category.

Kiss My Advice: The best advice is trust your own advice. Keep developing your grasp of humor to deal with all the bad advice, no matter where it comes from.

Have an Awful Day: Brighten someone's day by bypassing the familiar and meaningless "have a nice day". Replace it with a saying that will wake them up and put a smile on their face. Say it with conviction and wait for their response and hold... this is a great way to see if they are listening.

He's Not Such a Bad Guy / I Thought She Was Horrible When I Met Her: We have all made such statements. And often after taking the time to get to know the person, our first impression was proven wrong. Humor keeps us eternally open for surprises... humor keeps things new, young, and fun.

Hide and Seek: Humor is always searching for the truth. For all ages this game never changes. Adults just feel compelled to make the rules more severe and serious. Humor breaks down, cuts through all pretension and dissension.

Hollywood: The most selfish, self-absorbed, checked out, lonesome, rigid, dead people interact with the most creative, playful, loving, caring people that feed the world their entertainment. What contrast, what sadness, what laughs!

How Do You Do That Thing You Do?: We are all good at something. Whatever one's "thing" may be, it is difficult, if not impossible, to explain how they do that thing they do. This is because it has evolved, you have evolved, and it has become "second nature" to you now. No matter who you are, what your thing is, the ability to laugh at yourself for the thing you do should become second nature to you as well. This will improve that thing you do exponentially.

I Can't Remember Anything, Until it is Time to Remember Everything: Everything great is in us from the get go, so go out into the world and share your greatness, not your sadness, pain, misery, anger, frustration, and fears. Human terrorism is practiced in our day-to-day inhuman encounters; there is a psychological war that is being played out in our society that is insidious and hideous. And we are all guilty of perpetrating it on one another. Bring your best game, not your worst game, out into the streets.

I Like My Pain Straight: Pain makes us stupid, it makes us sad, it frustrates us, makes us angry, yet it is inevitable throughout life. Ironic, isn't it?

I Once Had a Great Thought, But I Forgot What it Was: Humor and laughter work really well for all the frustration that is ahead of you in life.

If Ignorance is Bliss, than is Awareness Painful?: Yes. Because awareness contains truth, and truth scares the shit out of us, but without truth how can you transcend your painful awareness. Besides, ignorance is not bliss, it's death.

It's like, you know, whatever...: Is this a sentence? Never use this title, or any part of this title when applying for a job, you know?

Innate Fears: Humor is a fear buster, and you're in charge of how many fears you need or want to keep.

It is Not the Clothes That Make the Man: Or the watch, or the car, or the house, or the job... it is the sense of humor, and a daily practice of foolosophy.

Life Should be Lived, Not Analyzed: A life without reflection is not worth living, but nothing is worse than being trapped in one's head, trapped in a rut, or fear bound.

Lifeable: To be able at life. To be able to live.

Little Head, Big Head: Gentlemen, don't let your little head do all the thinking for your big head. Once your little head makes a mistake, it is your big head that has to do the recovering and rebounding.

Los Angeles: Modern-day Rome

Making Fun of Oneself: In fact, do not stop there, make fun of as many things as you possibly can. Every human being likes to have fun, however, we naturally have different ideas of fun.

Mirror Time: Here is something you can limit to 11 seconds! You know what you look like silly... so just go out and play!

Never Grow Up: The best advice we can give all children is to never grow up, meaning keep the best parts of your natural childlike spirit.

No Patience... Become Patient: Whatever happened to the saying, "Good things come to those who wait"? When we only have an 11 second attention span, we lack the patience to cultivate these life-affirming emotional necessities. It is not surprising everybody needs therapy... Try comedy therapy and stick around!

Outlets: The more the merrier

Personal Freedom: Freedom is fun, yet no one can obtain it without a good understanding of our greatest gift. Begin by laughing at your subconscious mind.

Playing Hurt: Like an athlete, remember that LIFE IS A SERIES OF COMEBACKS. Humor is the elixir while in rehab. Like ice on your knee, humor in your head and heart eases the pain and helps you heal.

Pure Silliness: Experience total abandon, jump into the abyss... set yourself free with silliness.

Push People's Buttons: To learn, grow, feel, laugh, and of course have fun, push those buttons! Through other's expressions, body language and attitude, the child is alerted to their emotional wardrobe... Are they wearing a bikini, a pair of shorts, or a suit of armor? Through fun, play, silliness, and humor, the striptease begins. Help others by pushing the buttons that allow the clothes to fall off.

Raising Parents: Responsibility can be fun, playful, and healthy when humor is involved. All children have a huge responsibility to remind their parents of when the role-playing is becoming too serious. This is when the children do not have enough room to play, grow, feel, or function. No parent in their right mind wants to kill their child's nature. Use humor in all judgments because real maturity is the ability to smile and laugh at yourself, when you have made an incorrect judgment. Keep humor as the mediator between yourself and all others.

Ripped and Lonely: What good is a flat stomach with a fat head?

Seriosity: Would like to see this in Webster's dictionary. The meaning is – a person is serious about the thing, subject they're talking about, but they don't take it so seriously that they can't really listen and be open to more learning on the subject. It usually begins the sentence, "In all seriosity..."

Spiritual Bankruptcy: Once upon a time, F. Scott Fitzgerald referred to us as shallow, superficial, and spiritually bankrupt. You can go to church, synagogue, or any establishment or gathering, but this does not necessarily make you a spiritual being. Spirits are attracted to the laughter of children.

Speak for Yourself: We all leave school, home, socially emotionally retarded. Do not be afraid of the truth, and please embrace this generalization about us.

Sticks and Stones: An oldie but goodie... No one can put you down but you, no one can label you but you, and to quote Eleanor Roosevelt[39], "No one can make you feel inferior without your consent."

Stop The World, I Want To Get Off: A couple of things we know for certain in today's hectic, insane world: Our sense of humor is tested 24/7; Like it or not, this is a pass/fail exam.

Take Everything as a Compliment: One of the major tenants of foolosophy. Humor teaches us to take everything as a compliment for we truly do not know where a person is coming from much of the time. And if you do know where they are coming from then that is your excuse for not taking it personally. Either way, life is much funnier this way.

Taking Oneself Out of the Equation: This is the art of listening.

Talking Up to People: Use humor to play small so you can see where other people stand. Discipline is freedom, and much of the time we have to know what to overlook, but not ignore. Let people impress you if they need to, never let them depress you.

The Ability to Hang: Whether alone or with others, the ability to just be...

The Age of Sedation: Ritalin for young children, Prozac for PMS, and the general public self-medicating just to get by. Use 'H' (humor) as your drug of choice and the others will become unnecessary.

The Art of Laughing at Oneself: At any moment in the day, you may have true liberation, simply by laughing at the fact you are having negative thoughts.

---

39. Fortune Cookie

The Art of Teasing: Enjoy criticism while learning. Affection and attention are the two most important elements when showering a loved one, or foe, with good-humored honesty that is called "teasing". Through teasing, even personal attacks of an unfriendly kind can be diffused and used to one's advantage.

The Bottom Line: Please refrain from using either of these. Life is not a damn business and you are a lot more than a number.

The Capacious Mind: Meaning "roomy, able to hold much". This is the expanding consciousness that we all aspire to. In fact, you might say it is the reason we are here. This is humor's gift back to the user. Your mind will thank you for it, as will your heart!

The Child's Mind: What is good and great in all of us must be preserved. It keeps us most curious and interested, as well as playful, fun, and interesting. All children can laugh at themselves. This is the clean slate, the purity of the child's mind. Humor runs free, and keeps the idea of play and fun totally alive and well. As we get larger, things want to kill the play and fun. A well developed sense of humor is the key to life. Make no mistake about it, we are here to play, have fun, uncover and discover more and more about what it means to be human.

The Consummate Actor: We are all actors on the world-stage. Make sure to play your part.

The Cosmic Joke: YOU ARE HERE.

The Critic: We live in a world of criticism, and this is never, ever going to change. But you can adjust, adapt, advance using humor to make all criticism a learning thing, a positive thing in time. Once you stop choking on criticism and realize that no one can put you down but you, you are in the throes of humor. This is how you learn to take everything as a compliment. Remember, everyone has a large desire to be right, to feel superior, even if they know they are not. People who criticize with the intention of putting another down are the funniest, most obvious morons of all. So just play along, keep a smiling mind, and do not buy into their criticism.

The Day I Lost My Sense of Humor: Hopefully you never use this title.

The Fountain of Youth: No matter what age you are, no matter where you are, or what you're doing or not doing, you can be any age you want. Humor is not new-age or old-age, it's ageless. It puts all time on your side, for it teaches us the importance of laughing at physical demise, thereby easing the mind, knowing that it is mind over matter.

The Great Healer: HUMOUR.

The Great Teacher: PAIN.

The Last Frontier: Conquering oneself is the object of humor.

The Loss of Spontaneity: Hopefully this hasn't happened. If a friend calls you at the last minute, be ready and available for fun. Make fun your first priority and responsibility. Your kids will love you for it, people will love you for it.

The Missing Link: Life is a series of comebacks; humor is the link to make it possible. You should always smile and laugh at any negative to bring about freedom and light. Humor is the ultimate release valve for the pressure of life.

The Phone Message: Please be creative for fun's sake! Example: "Hello, just leave your shoe size, hair color, and what you had for dinner last night, and let me guess who's calling..."

The Simple Truth: Humor is it. It is all about the future, for it is the best way to view the past.

The Sixth Sense: Increase all other senses with the most important sense... a sense of humor. Can you see it?

The Universe at Play: Think and substitute the word play for the words work, love, and life.

There's Definitely Something Wrong With Me: Self-deprecating humor is enjoyed by everyone so practice making fun of your defects, flaws, foibles, shortcomings, daily amongst friends and acquaintances, they will love you for it.

To Good At Ignoring One Another: Here's something we are getting too good at in our daily activities, for we are now a culture of fear and we are all feeling the crunch.

Too Quick to Qualify: Be not quick to qualify, for the laughs come to those who wait to hear the entire joke. Humor can be the equalizer that enables two very different points of view to find common ground. Use humor to break down and overcome all social barriers.

Trapped in One's Head: Modern mans worst disease.

You know, like, well, you know...: This and the above titles must be made fun of, no matter what the consequences are. More than half of America is using this unimaginative inarticulate syntax. Please catch anyone who is talking like this and mimic them.

You know what I mean? Because I don't

You know what I'm saying? Are you really listening to me? Because I'm so insecure I need to ask.

You're Never Going to Get It: This is true, but thanks to humor and your new ability to laugh at all labels of yourself, you're going to have a great time trying.

You're Not That Great: Humility is a beautiful thing, something we all need. Never take yourself so seriously that you believe your own greatness. This is the check and balance of humor that we all fall trap to.

We're All Underdogs: The ability to laugh at one's failures makes winners out of losers. Forgiveness, compassion, and empathy, begin with oneself. When you can honestly sincerely laugh at yourself, you will never lose again.

What Are We, Canned Goods?: It is perfectly normal to label people. Just remember, underneath that label is the same thing underneath yours. In the supermarket of life, try thinking of everyone as a child or a beautiful fool and give the attention, love, and understanding they need.

What to Say: To follow up on the mind to mouth principle... People are always trying to connect and communicate, but it is rare that we know what to say, or how to say it. Help me and you will help yourself in the struggle... Humor me and I will respond. What to say is the ability to be responsive rather than reactionary to whatever is occurring at that very moment... play with it as much as you can.

Whatever: One of the stupidest words in our language.

Write It Down, Get It Out: If bad thoughts enter you psyche, write them down. After a little time passes get together with a friend, family member, or even just yourself, and share them no matter how dark or upsetting they seem. Do not keep stuff on the inside, for there is much more room on the outside. This may be difficult at first, but once you get through the rough part, you will begin to see the humor in this, and never be bogged down again.

Appendix B

Reading People / Reading Books

Books are great, books are wonderful, but books were written by people. You won't be able to develop your sense of humor by simply reading, even absorbing this book. You must hit the streets, as scary as this might sound, and you must interact with as diverse a population of people as humanly possible. My life has been the richest life for this reason. In all my social emotional mental interaction it was my sense of play and sense of humor that made the game of life so much fun.

Books were given to me, handed to me, because people told me that I sounded like this person and that person. What a compliment! For when I read them I could appreciate the sensitivity, caring, and intelligence of the authors. Here is a short list of books used to inspire this one:

- A Course in Miracles by the FOUNDATION FOR INNER PEACE
- A Nietzsche Reader by R.J. Hollingdale
- A Natural History of the Senses by Diane Ackerman
- An Anthropologist on Mars by Oliver Sacks
- Anatomy of an Illness by Norman Cousins
- Audition by Michael Shurtleff
- Beyond Good and Evil by Friedrich Nietzsche

- Blink: The Power of Thinking Without Thinking by Malcolm Gladwell
- Comedy by George Meredith and Henri Bergson
- Dumbing Us Down by John Taylor Gatto
- Dumbth by Steve Allen
- Eccentrics: A Study of Sanity and Strangeness by Dr. David Weeks and Jamie James
- Escape From Freedom by Erich Fromm
- Everyone Poops by Taro Gomi
- Exuberance: The Passion for Life by Kay Redfield Jamison
- Free Play by Stephen Nachmanovitch
- Fools Are Everywhere by Beatrice Otto
- Genius by Harold Bloom
- Hole in our Soul by Martha Bayles
- Homo Ludens by Johan Huizinga
- How Proust Can Change Your Life by Alain de Botton
- How to Think like Leonardo da Vinci by Michael J. Gelb
- Ideas and Opinions by Albert Einstein
- Insight and Outlook by Arthur Koestler
- Is Sex Necessary? by James Thurber & E.B. White
- Laughing Matters by Lee Siegel
- Laughter by Robert R. Provine
- Life Against Death by Norman O. Brown
- Life and How to Survive It by Robin Skynner and John Cleese
- Linus Pauling: In His Own Words by Barbara Marinacci
- Mad as Hell: The Life and Work of Paddy Chayefsky by Shaun Considine
- Man's Search for Meaning by Viktor E. Frankl
- Mind Wide Open by Steven Johnson
- Mixed Nuts by Lawrence J. Epstein
- Nasty People by Jay Carter
- Now Dig This by Terry Southern
- Nothing But The Marvelous by Henry Miller
- Only The Truth Is Funny by Rick Reynolds
- Organizing Genius by Warren Bennis & Patricia Ward Biederman
- Out of My Life and Thought by Albert Schweitzer
- Oxymoronica by Dr. Mardy Grothe
- Picasso: In His Words by Hiro Clark
- Praise of Folly by Erasmus
- Psychotherapy East and West by Alan Watts
- Reviving Ophelia by Mary Pipher, Ph.D.
- School Girls: Young Women, Self-Esteem, and the Confidence Gap by Peggy Orenstein
- The Art of W.C. Fields by William K. Everson
- The Art Spirit by Robert Henri
- The Book: On the Taboo Against Knowing Who You Are by Alan Watts
- The Closing of the American Mind by Allan Bloom

- The Consolations of Philosophy by Alain de Botton
- The Culture of Fear by Barry Glassner
- The Drama of the Gifted Child by Alice Miller
- The End of Sanity by Martin L. Gross
- The Essential Crazy Wisdom by Wes "Scoop" Nisker
- The Human Zoo by Desmond Morris
- The Joyful Child by Peggy Jenkins, Ph.D.
- The Language Instinct: How the Mind Creates Language by Steven Pinker
- The Laurel & Hardy Theory of Consciousness by Colin Wilson
- The Little Book of Stress by Stuart and Linda Macfarlane
- The Morality of Laughter by F.H. Buckley
- The New Thought Police by Tammy Bruce
- The Portable Curmudgeon by Jon Winokur
- The Prosperous Few and The Restless Many by Noam Chomsky
- The Wisdom of Insecurity by Alan Watts
- There Are Men too Gentle to Live Among Wolves by James Kavanaugh
- Thou Shalt Not Be Aware by Alice Miller
- Touched With Fire by Kay Redfield Jamison
- Underdogs by Jim Dratfield
- Understanding Stupidity by James F. Welles, Ph.D.
- Why Read? by Mark Edmundson
- Wit & Wisdom by Oscar Wilde
- Woman: An Intimate Geography by Natalie Angier
- Women's Wit and Wisdom by Running Press
- You Just Don't Understand by Deborah Tannen, Ph.D.

In his own time, Jesus was considered a kook. He became a hero among the poor because he ministered to them, but respectable people probably saw him as a scruffy, wandering street person. Not only was Jesus labeled a fool, he sometimes accepted the role and deliberately played the fool as part of his radical protests.[40]
Wes "Scoop" Nisker,
The Essential Crazy Wisdom

---

40. The Essential Crazy Wisdom by Wes "Scoop" Nisker, Ten Speed Press, 2001

Books

Other Happy About Books

Purchase these books at Happy About
http://happyabout.info
or at other online and physical bookstores.

Learn About Men, Women and Relationships the Easy Way!.

The book describes the lessons and insights the three authors derived from their experiences and problems with men. Great tips, worth reading yourself and sharing with others.

Paperback:$14.95 164pgs
eBook: $11.95

Change Your Belief in Some Fundamental Tenants!

Learn more about the bible and christianity while getting challenged about some of the basic tenants.

Paperback:$16.95 140 pgs
eBook: $11.95

www.ingramcontent.com/pod-product-compliance
Lightning Source LLC
Chambersburg PA
CBHW071711090426
42738CB00009B/1736